Irving J. Gill, Architect

The author dedicates this book
to the memory of Esther McCoy.

We would like to thank the following
individuals and companies for their support of this book.

Staff and Trustees of Balboa Art Conservation Center
Bokal Kelley-Markham Architects
Mr. & Mrs. E. Scofield Bonnet
Buck Fine Arts
Mr. & Mrs. Everett G. Jackson
Mr. & Mrs.* Philip M. Klauber
Mr. & Mrs. Josiah L. Neeper
Beth Paynter Fund, San Diego Community Foundation
Sarah W. Spiess
John M. and Sally B. Thornton Foundation
David Huot West

*posthumously

Irving J. Gill, Architect

BRUCE KAMERLING

"Any deviation from simplicity
results in a loss of dignity."

SAN DIEGO
HISTORICAL
SOCIETY

A PUBLICATION OF THE SAN DIEGO HISTORICAL SOCIETY
1993

Printed in the United States of America

PUBLISHED BY

San Diego Historical Society

P.O. Box 81825

San Diego, California 92138

EDITOR

Richard Crawford

COPY EDITOR

Robert Carlton

DESIGN AND PRODUCTION SUPERVISION

Jill Maxwell Berry

PRINTING

Conklin Litho

Library of Congress Cataloging-in-Publication Data

Kamerling, Bruce A.,
    Irving J. Gill, architect / Bruce Kamerling
      p. cm.
    Includes bibliographical references and index.
    ISBN 0-918740-16-9 (pbk. : acid. free)
    1. Gill, Irving, 1870-1936. 2. Architects—California—Biography,
3. Eclecticism in architecture—California, Southern.   I. Gill,
Irving, 1870-1936. II.Title.
NA737.G53K36   1993
720'.92—dc20
[B]   93-36417
                                CIP

ILLUSTRATION CREDITS:

Cover: Irving Gill rendering for a guest cottage for Wheeler J. Bailey, La Jolla (1932), San Diego Historical Society, Architectural Records Collection, gift of Helen Reynolds.

Architectural Concrete for Small Buildings: 121 (bottom)

Ken Arnone: 36 (bottom)

Bar Harbor Historical Society: 29 (bottom)

Craftsman: 75, 79 (bottom)

David Hewitt/Anne Garrison: 8, 73 (bottom), 116, 117

Historic American Buildings Survey (photographs by Marvin Rand): 48, 96 (bottom), 97, 100 (bottom), 104 (bottom), 106 (top)

House Beautiful: 27 (bottom)

Long Beach Public Library: 105

National Park Service, Frederick Law Olmsted National Historic Site: 28, 29 (top)

Oceanside Historical Society: 118 (bottom), 119 (bottom)

Marvin Rand: 57 (top), 101

Santa Fe Springs, City of: 108

University of California Santa Barbara, University Art Museum, Architectural Drawing Collection: 4, 25 (bottom), 42 (top), 43, 45 (top), 57 (bottom), 61 (bottom), 62 (top), 66 (bottom), 70, 71, 73 (top), 74, 77, 79 (top), 82, 83, 85, 89 (bottom), 94 (bottom), 95 (bottom), 96 (center), 106 (bottom), 107 (top)

All other images are from the San Diego Historical Society Photograph Collection, many of which were contributed by the descendants of Gill clients.

Contents

Preface

In an essay on Frank Lloyd Wright published two years before Gill's death (in *Art in America in Modern Times*, 1934), the prominent critic and architectural historian Henry-Russell Hitchcock, Jr., gave Gill high praise: "Except for Irving Gill in California, who created out of a radical simplification of Spanish Colonial design a modern treatment of poured concrete construction for houses, Wright has been the only modern architect of consequence of the first quarter of the century in America." Even Wright, who would have been annoyed at being placed in the same class with anyone, begrudgingly admitted in *Genius and the Mobocracy* (1949) that "[Gill's] work was a kind of elimination which if coupled with a finer sense of proportion would have been—I think it was, anyway—a real contribution to our so-called modern movement."

Sadly, time has not been kind to Gill's legacy. For an architect greatly concerned with permanence, it is shocking to see how much of his work has been destroyed in less than a century. The majority of his finest residences—including the Dodge, Scripps, Timken, Klauber, Banning, Laughlin, Darst, and Barker houses—are all gone. Because the spare simplicity of Gill's work so easily lent itself to additions, many of those buildings that remain have suffered the indignities of added-on mansard tile roofs, superfluous wrought iron, and irrelevant moldings—all the things he so desperately wanted to discourage.

Gill's legacy is further hurt by a lack of documentary evidence. Almost no personal papers are known that might give us a deeper understanding of Gill the man. A large group of his drawings is preserved in the Architectural Records Collection at the University of California, Santa Barbara, and a smaller collection in the San Diego Historical Society's archives, but these files cover less than a third of Gill's known projects. The original drawings for the Dodge house, which Ada Louise Huxtable (*New York Times*, March 8, 1970) called "one of the fifteen most significant houses in the history of American domestic architecture," have not been located. Too much of Gill's work can now be appreciated only through historical photographs, and many designs do not survive even in that fragile medium.

Even so, much has been learned about Gill since Esther McCoy's pioneering research of the 1950s, which resulted in her chapter on Gill in *Five California Architects*. I first began compiling data on Gill twenty years ago, with no particular purpose in mind other than satisfying my personal interest. Taking on the task of reviewing thousands of unindexed microfilms of the San Diego papers, I turned up a great deal of new information. Contacting the descendants of Gill clients, I was able to assemble at the San Diego Historical Society an extensive photographic record of Gill's work.

In 1978 William Chandler, then Associate Curator of Decorative Arts at the San Diego Museum of Art, asked me to submit a proposal for an Irving Gill exhibit at the museum with myself acting as guest curator. The exhibit, which ran from March 30 to May 20, 1979, included original drawings, historical photographs, and more recent photographs by Marvin Rand. I asked Esther McCoy to give a lecture during the run of the exhibit, which she did on April 26, Gill's 109th birthday. At that time, and on subsequent visits, I discussed with her the need for an updated book about Gill. She encouraged me to pursue this task, with this admonition: "Make sure your work is your own."

History, however, cannot be written in a vacuum. Historians must rely on many sources for their information, and I have been fortunate in the help provided me by numerous friends and colleagues over the years. When it became known that I was compiling data about Gill, other researchers were generous when their labors turned up relevant information while exploring other subjects. I would particularly like to thank Susan Carrico, Kathy Flanigan, Nick Follansbee, Roger Hatheway, Joseph Musil, Pat Schaelchlin, and Karna Webster. Betty Quayle conducted genealogical research on Gill for me in Syracuse while working on her own family tree, and I am grateful for her help. Additional assistance came from Gill's grandnephew, Rev. John Gill, and the descendants of many Gill clients who have provided information over the years.

Finally, I must acknowledge with deep appreciation the assistance and cooperation of David Gebhard and Marvin Rand; although both have discussed working on a Gill book with me, because of our difficult schedules this has not yet been possible. Special thanks are due to Mr. Rand for allowing me to use some of his excellent photographs, even though he is planning his own pictorial study of Gill in the near future, a volume to be greatly anticipated.

The present book, which marks the one-hundredth anniversary of Gill's arrival in San Diego, is not intended to be a definitive biography. Too much information is lacking, particularly concerning Gill's years in Los Angeles, for that study to be written at the present time. My main purpose has been to assemble as much accurate data as possible in a convenient, well-illustrated format without unnecessarily duplicating material adequately covered by Esther McCoy. Unless otherwise noted, all Gill quotations are taken from his article "The Home of the Future" reprinted in Appendix B. Appendix A reproduces his article "New Ideas About Concrete Floors." In both of these appendices the original punctuation and spelling have been retained. Appendix C contains a list of known Gill projects including the location and present status when known.

I hope that I have succeeded in correcting old errors without adding any new ones; but that may be inevitable, so I apologize in advance.

Bruce Kamerling
Curator of Collections
San Diego Historical Society

Irving Gill about age 19.

The Early Years

Irving Gill descended from a Quaker family that had emigrated from London about 1700 and settled in New Jersey. By the mid-nineteenth century, Gill's ancestors had migrated to the rural community of Tully, about twenty miles south of Syracuse in central New York. Here Gill's parents, Joseph and Cynthia (Scullen) Gill, established a farm. Joseph later listed himself as a carpenter and also worked as a building contractor in a small way. Several other members of the Gill family were involved in the building trades.

Irving John Gill was born at Tully on April 26, 1870, one of six children (Mary Louella, John David, Francis B., Charles L., and Floyd). As a youth, Gill, known as "Jack" in the family, attended the Madison Street School in Syracuse. By 1887-88 he listed himself as a gardener in the Syracuse city directory, and his later interest in the relationship between architecture and landscape may date to these early years.

In the 1889-90 Syracuse city directory, Gill identified his occupation as "draftsman," and other sources reveal that he was employed in the architectural office of Ellis G. Hall. (Years later, Gill employed an Ellis G. Hall, either this same architect or his son, as a draftsman on the George Marston house and other projects.) According to Gill's nephew Louis, Irving was always the family hero "because he adventured into the far West—Chicago." By 1890, Gill obtained employment in the Chicago office of Joseph L. Silsbee, who had been Hall's partner before departing from Syracuse in 1884. Silsbee, also Frank Lloyd Wright's first employer, helped introduce the Shingle style in the Midwest.

By 1891 Gill had moved to the office of Dankmar Adler and Louis Sullivan in Chicago, where Frank Lloyd Wright was then employed as chief draftsman. According to Wright, he personally hired Gill as one of his "squad." Sullivan advocated the abandonment of European revival styles of architecture in favor of the development of a national, democratic style, and encouraged his students to study primitive architectural forms. He also endorsed the principle of organic architecture: that form generates from within and that a building must express both the physical and social aspects of the environment from which it developed. These concepts he later summarized in his now-famous dictum "Form ever follows function. This is the law."

This must have been an exciting time for a young man interested in a career in architecture, and Gill was deeply influenced by the training he received in Sullivan's office. Gill joined the architectural staff of the World's Columbian Exposition and presumably took part in the creation of Sullivan's Transportation Building for the fair. Not one to hold back, Gill worked so hard that he literally made himself seriously ill, and he was forced to leave the exposition project before the fair opened in May of 1893. Louis Gill later recalled this about his uncle's departure from Chicago: "As he told me, downhearted and discouraged, he decided to get as far away as possible from the scene of his failure." (The egocentric Wright's later claim that Gill left because of a critical remark he had made can probably be discounted.)

Why Gill chose San Diego is not known, although the city's health-giving climate had been widely proclaimed by many promoters. Sullivan had visited San Diego in 1889 and may have encouraged his young draftsman to take advantage of the opportunities that Southern California afforded. San Diego in 1893 was no longer the bustling boom town it had been in the late 1880s. Completion of the California Southern Railroad in 1885 had finally provided San Diego with a direct link to the East, causing an unprecedented land boom. Drawn both by the mild climate and potential real estate investment, the population skyrocketed from fewer than 5,000 in 1885 to about 40,000 in 1887. Many were forced to live and work in tents while numerous new homes, hotels, and business blocks were being constructed in the most fashionable Queen Anne, Italianate, and Second Empire styles.

Unfortunately, as with so many booms, the bubble burst as quickly as it had grown, and by 1888 people could not leave town fast enough. By 1890 the population had stabilized at about 16,000, but things were far from good. A nationwide financial depression in 1893 saw five out of the eight banks in San Diego close their doors, and many people had their life savings and investments wiped out almost overnight. The 1887 San Diego city directory listed fourteen architectural firms working in San Diego. By 1893 there were only four. In the middle of this uncertain period, Irving Gill arrived in San Diego.

Evidently, San Diego's famous climate worked rapidly on Gill, and he recovered from his illness. Before long, he set up an office in Room 19 of the Pierce-Morse Block, one of the more impressive edifices constructed during San Diego's brief boom period. An article about the building's tenants in the August 1893 issue of *The Golden Era* is prophetic:

> Mr. Gill intends nothing short of revolutionizing the country architecture of this fair "Italy" of ours. Many of his graceful and suitable designs are already in the hands of the carpenter. We wish Mr. Gill every success and hope the time is not far distant when many such will take the place of the tall, uncongenial edifices that rudely suggest blizzards and snows in this harmonious land of eternal summer.

Although sources indicate that Gill was reporting "great activity in building," few projects from this period are known. Sometime in the summer or fall of 1894, Gill went into partnership with Joseph Falkenham, a prominent architect of Queen Anne style homes. Little is known of Falkenham's personal life other than what he

Louis Sullivan's Transportation Building at the World's Columbian Exposition, Chicago (1893).

recorded on his voter registration form dated August 17, 1894. He listed his age as thirty-nine, his occupation as architect and builder, and his birthplace as Ohio. Beyond this, newspaper accounts indicate that he was a very prolific architect in both Coronado and San Diego. The 1890 San Diego city directory identified him as a member of the Board of Public Works with an office in City Hall.

It appears that Falkenham left San Diego for a time, probably because of the economic situation. The August 20, 1892, *Coronado Evening Mercury* states that he had relocated to San Francisco with an office in the Phelan Block on Market Street. The *San Diego Union* of June 5, 1893, printed an announcement from the *Los Angeles Herald* that he had opened an office in that city. Either finding opportunities no better to the north or deciding that there might be less competition for jobs in San Diego, he returned. By May 1894 he had an impressive list of projects at hand, including two large business blocks.

Falkenham must have found it desirable to take on a partner in order to complete the many projects facing him. The September 3, 1894, *San Diego Union* published a list of buildings and remodeling projects being undertaken by "Falkenham & Gill, the architects." Among these was the Gerichten-Choate-Peterson Block at 832 Fifth Avenue, where they established their office. This building featured the largest plate-glass windows in San Diego. In 1895 Falkenham left San Diego once again, this time permanently, and where he went next is not known.

It seems likely that most of the Falkenham & Gill projects mentioned in the *Union* article were already under way when Gill was taken on as partner. In one of them, however—a residence for Major Miles Moylan—several features point to the hand of the young Gill. Major Moylan led a colorful military career before retiring to San Diego about 1893. A captain in Reno's battalion, he was among the few survivors of the Battle of the Little Big Horn. Moylan was also in the Battle of Wounded Knee, for which he received the Congressional Medal of Honor for bravery. His residence was designed in an appropriately patriotic Colonial Revival style, certainly a departure from Falkenham's earlier work. The distinctive broken-bed pediments and grouped porch columns were used by Gill on other early projects. The most telling bit of evidence pointing to Gill's hand is the entry hall newel post, which is notable for the openwork designs of Sullivanesque tracery in its inset panels.

On his own again, Gill came to the attention of some important clients. Large homes for David K. Horton, G. George Garrettson, and Abel H. Frost, as well as an unusual music chamber for Ralph Granger, helped establish him as one of San Diego's most important young architects. Built in a variety of styles, these early projects indicate that Gill was attempting to find an architectural form appropriate to Southern California. Starting in the mid-1890s, his experiments with the use of concrete eventually led to important contributions in concrete construction methods and design possibilities. Without academic training, Gill had developed into a remarkably talented and innovative architect.

Gill established his first San Diego office in the Pierce-Morse Block at Sixth and F, designed by Nelson Comstock and Carl Trotsche in 1887.

Gill's first project in San Diego, the Daniel Schuyler
residence (1893), gives little evidence of the direction
his work was to take after the turn of the century.
Neoclassical elements include the broken-bed pediments
and Ionic columns. The scroll-cut brackets and octagonal
shingles are holdovers from the Victorian era.

At Hillside in El Cajon, Gill created a more unusual residence (1893) for John Kendall, a newcomer from England. The local press identified the style as "East Indian bungalow" because of the low profile and exotic roofline. The decorative woodwork of the gables in contrasting colors created the impression of half-timbering. Diamond-pane windows and a cozy inglenook gave the interior the feeling of an English cottage.

Looking north on Fifth Avenue from F Street, ca. 1895.
On the corner is the five-story Keating Block completed in
1891 by Gill's future partner, William Hebbard. Next to it
is the Gerichten-Choate-Peterson Building, designed by
Falkenham & Gill (1894). The architects maintained their
office in the structure, which featured the largest plate-
glass windows in San Diego.

Gill designed this rambling bungalow for Gail Nichols in Coronado about 1895. The view from the broad veranda stretched all the way to Mexico. Gill's earliest known rendering, it demonstrates the painterly style he maintained throughout his career.

The bold geometry of the David K. Horton house in National City (1895) shows that Gill had an early interest in streamlining architecture. The interior featured a large and beautifully arranged reception room, and the kitchen had a skylight.

The gambrel roof of the G. George Garrettson house (1896) shows a debt to the Shingle style of Joseph L. Silsbee. Among the structure's distinctive elements are a side entrance through the chimney on the east and a fireplace under a staircase in the main entry hall. The stair hall, finished in Port Orford cedar, includes an elaborately carved handrail terminus as well as a landing with perfectly square stick balusters.

When Ralph Granger struck it rich in the silver mines of
Colorado, he indulged a long-held dream and purchased
an entire collection of rare violins. To house the priceless
collection, Granger had Gill design a private recital hall
(1896) next to his home in National City. The ceiling was
designed without columns that might obstruct the sound
effects, and the floor was also specifically supported to
create the best acoustical properties. In effect, the room
itself acted as a musical sound box. At one end, a large
concrete vault contained a safe to protect the King
Joseph, Stradivarii, and other fine instruments. Gill
attended the first performance on August 20, 1896.
Two years later, the original structure was greatly
expanded. The problem of tying the addition to the
original chamber without ruining the lighting of the
clerestory windows resulted in an interlocking roofline of
Japanese-like simplicity. The addition features a ceiling
mural of Euterpe, Muse of Music, painted by Detlef
Sammann, and an elaborate organ screen, the design of
which shows the influence of Louis Sullivan.

The house Gill designed for Abel H. Frost (1896) is strongly Neo-Georgian in character. The symmetrical façade has a frontispiece climbing three levels to a dormer with swans-neck scrolls. To offset the perfect symmetry, a chimney on the west balances a covered porch on the east. The interior, in Port Orford cedar, contains a large entry hall and spacious rooms.

Hebbard & Gill, Architects

William Sterling Hebbard (1863-1930).

After working independently for nearly two years, Gill became the partner of William Sterling Hebbard in December of 1896. One of the few architects to remain in San Diego during the economic panic of the early 1890s, Hebbard brought sound academic training to the partnership. Hebbard was born on April 16, 1863, in Milford, Michigan, where his family owned a woolen mill. Spending his youth in Michigan, Hebbard later attended the School of Architecture at Cornell University. After being graduated in 1887, he traveled to Heidelberg, Germany.

Returning from Europe, Hebbard became a draftsman for the architectural firm of Burnham & Root in Chicago. Daniel H. Burnham and John W. Root established their firm in 1873, only two years after the Chicago fire. This infamous disaster cleared the slate and created the need for stricter building codes. These restrictions opened the door for the development of advanced construction methods and a new design vocabulary. Burnham & Root were among the most prominent architects in Chicago, and their work must have left a lasting impression on young Hebbard.

Moving west in 1888, Hebbard briefly worked as a draftsman for Curlett, Eisen and Cuthbertson in Los Angeles. Later that year, he received the commission to design a powerhouse for San Diego's short-lived cable railroad system. Relocating to San Diego, Hebbard established himself as an independent architect. About 1890, he became an associate of James, Merritt, and W. E. Reid. Among the most important architects in San Diego at the time, the Reid Brothers had been brought from Evansville, Indiana, to design Hotel del Coronado in 1886. About 1890, the Reid Brothers relocated to San Francisco, and Hebbard became the successor to their San Diego business, moving into their offices in the First National Bank Building.

Hebbard inherited a number of unfinished Reid Brothers projects, including the Keating Block and the Fisher Opera House, both of which featured two lower floors of Richardsonian stone work topped by three floors of pressed brick. Hebbard designed several English-style churches in Coronado and San Diego, and a Neo-Georgian summer home for Col. Jesse Root Grant, son of Ulysses S. Grant. Certainly Hebbard and Gill would have known of each other's work. They announced the establishment of their firm in December 1896 and set up offices in the Grant Block, where they remained for the duration of their partnership.

Two of their first large projects, the Los Baños bathhouse and the State Normal School, derived from buildings constructed for the Chicago world's fair. Although Los Baños was basically Hispano-Moresque in character, the arch-within-a-rectangle entrance and terrace pavilions were directly inspired by Sullivan's Transportation Building at the fair. Charles B. Atwood's Palace of Fine Arts provided the model for the Normal School, with its rows of Ionic columns and Neoclassical details.

Other influences were also evident in the firm's early work. Hebbard & Gill constructed many residences in the English style that ranged from large brick mansions to half-timbered cottages, often with massive stone foundations. A large wooden home for Gen. Mendell C. Churchill showed a definite Japanese inspiration. In 1900 the Landmarks Club of California hired Hebbard & Gill to stabilize the ruins of the Mission San Diego de Alcalá and the influence of the Mission style began to be felt in their subsequent work. Gill spent many hours measuring and studying the missions. According to Louis Gill, "He was much impressed, not with their sentimental appeal or the heaviness of the construction, but with their straightforward simplicity, the economy in the use of materials and their frank declaration that buildings should be made for use."

Hebbard's stature as an architect was greatly enhanced when Governor Henry T. Gage appointed him to the first State Architectural Board in 1901. A law regulating the practice of architecture was enacted on March 21, 1901; it required that anyone calling himself an architect had to pass an examination by the board and obtain a certificate. The law allowed that any architect engaged in the practice of architecture when the act was passed would automatically be granted a certificate without examination, and Gill obtained his certificate on March 23, 1901. California was only the second state (after Illinois) to pass such a law.

In 1903 the Chamber of Commerce established a Hotel Committee for the purpose of trying to build a modern hotel on the site occupied by the aging Horton House hotel, which had been constructed in 1870. The *San Diego Union* of March 18, 1903, reported that Gill had been named a special member of the committee, an indication of his growing prestige. "He is now in the east at work on certain projects other than a hotel for San Diego, but as he will meet people whom he might interest in the project, the committee proposes that he shall speak with authority as a representative of the chamber of commerce, and that the chamber will back up what he says." Hebbard & Gill, in association with Edward G. Kent of Los Angeles, began preparing designs for the hotel in 1905. The U. S. Grant Hotel, ultimately designed by Harrison Albright, opened its doors in 1910.

Harrison Albright had been a strong advocate of reinforced concrete construction. In December 1905 he delivered a paper on reinforced concrete before the Southern California chapter of the American Institute of Architects in Los Angeles. Albright covered the strength and safety of the material as well as its fire-resistant qualities. It is not known if Gill attended this lecture, but the December 16 *San Diego Union* gave it extensive coverage. The following year, the disastrous San Francisco earthquake made architects aware of how inadequate many of the current building methods were in the face of natural disasters. On April 26

Irving Gill (rear center) teaching a class in architectural
drawing at the San Diego YMCA in 1906.

the *Union* reported that the buildings which best survived the earthquake were constructed of reinforced concrete. Although Gill had already been using concrete for about ten years, these accounts must have made him even more convinced of the material's potential.

Little is known about Gill's personal life. A notice in the *Union* of March 20, 1898, mentions a "tally-ho" party that Gill hosted at the Granger Music Hall, where his guests enjoyed "a delightful musicale." Gill also joined the San Diego Rowing Club and remained an active member until he departed for Los Angeles. Rev. John Gill, the architect's grandnephew, wrote that "...he was quite a handsome man who was very much in demand in the social life of San Diego. His name was continuously linked (by the gossips) with this belle and that one. The Coronado Hotel was his social stamping ground where he charmed a succession of the ladies. Apparently, he never took any of it seriously; he was amused by it, but basically I think he was much happier alone. He did not need people."

Through these social contacts, particularly Easterners wintering at Hotel del Coronado, Gill obtained commissions to design several large homes in Rhode Island and Maine between 1900 and 1905. He traveled cross-country several times to supervise construction and must certainly have visited friends and former associates in Chicago on one or more of these trips. There he would have been exposed to the newly emerging Prairie style, with its emphasis on straight lines and a low profile. Beginning in 1905, the influence of the Prairie style became evident in several Hebbard & Gill projects, particularly the homes for Alice Lee, Katherine Teats, Mary Cossitt and Frederick Burnham on Seventh Avenue.

Like many San Diegans, Gill dabbled in various forms of investment. In 1900 he and seven others filed a placer mining claim for the "Never Fail Mine" in San Diego County. Both Hebbard and Gill were among the original subscribers to the San Diego Securities and Trust Company in 1905. Perhaps more appropriately, Gill began to purchase real estate and eventually owned lots in the Sherman Heights and Hillcrest neighborhoods of San Diego. Beginning about 1900, he began to use this property to construct experimental cottages. Here he applied some of his new ideas about design and construction and then lived in the cottages himself to test their feasibility.

Although Hebbard & Gill had designed some very large homes for some very wealthy clients, Gill was becoming increasingly aware of the potential that architecture had for social reform. He was convinced that a well-designed and well-constructed home could become a vehicle for change. On the back of a photograph of a pair of experimental cottages, Gill wrote this proud note:

Dear Father:

These are two small houses that Charles built for me last winter: I built them so as to work out some new ideas I had for a cheap, semi-fire proof cottage for working mens families: They have been a great success & I am building several others of this same construction.

Opposite page: The first major project to confront the new architectural firm of Hebbard & Gill was the design of a large bathhouse (1897) for Graham Babcock, son of Hotel del Coronado builder Elisha Babcock. The incentive for building the bathhouse was the availability of a free supply of hot water: the heated seawater created during the cooling of exhaust steam from the giant Corliss engine that ran the dynamo powering the streetcar system. Rather than return the heated water to the bay, Babcock decided to construct a salt-water plunge next door to the power plant. Later named "Los Baños," the structure had a glass roof and a rather fanciful Hispano-Moresque façade. The entrance and terrace pavilions were directly inspired by Sullivan's Transportation Building, except that here starfish, dolphins, tridents, and other appropriately aquatic elements were used for ornamentation instead of Sullivan's elaborate traceries.

Harr Wagner, editor of *The Golden Era* magazine, had been advocating the establishment of a teachers' college in San Diego since 1889. Finally, in December of 1897, a call for plans for a $100,000 Normal School was announced. In January of the following year, the Hebbard & Gill plans—drawn by Gill—were selected over those from seven other architectural firms from San Diego, Los Angeles, and Texas. Because of funding limitations, construction took place in three phases. The center section containing five classrooms and an assembly hall was dedicated on May 1, 1899. The east wing was added in 1900, but the west wing was not completed until 1904. Gill modeled his design after the Fine Arts building at the Chicago world's fair of 1893. Mercifully, the pediments representing historical and allegorical subjects and pedestals for statuary that had been suggested in the original plan were eliminated in the final design.

One of Hebbard & Gill's first large houses in the English
style, the Anson P. Stephens residence (1898) in
Coronado, had a broadly sweeping gable covering two
floors. The house was altered by Frank Mead and Richard
Requa in 1917 and greatly enlarged by Louis Gill in
1922.

The Coronado home of Gen. Mendell C. Churchill and his
niece Mary C. Pratt (1898) had a distinct oriental
character. A multi-hipped roof with low pitch and broad
eaves is evidence of the clients' interest in Japanese
design. Before starting the house, the owners traveled to
Japan, where they purchased furnishings and cherrywood
lumber for the interiors. The architects positioned the
house on its triangular lot in such a way that every room
received sunlight for part of each day.

Hebbard & Gill's first use of Spanish architecture for a residence was in the comfortable home they designed for John H. Kleine in Lakeside in 1897-98. The vine-covered pergola and smooth stucco walls with clean openings were to become familiar Gill devices. About 1905-06, Gill designed a smaller house for Kleine in his more modern style. This may have been a wedding present for his daughter, Elsa, who married Ralph Johnson in 1905. Gill attended the couple's wedding.

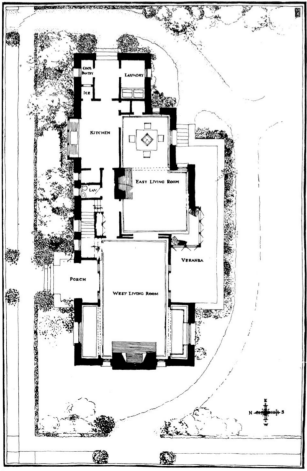

The "Granite Cottage" (1900) designed for Waldo and Hazel Waterman had half-timbered gables and massive granite-block construction. In order to simplify housework, the architects made much of the interior woodwork flush with the plaster to eliminate dust-catching ledges. Gill was impressed with Hazel's ability to grasp architectural concepts; after her husband died in 1903, she took a correspondence course in architectural drafting, and Gill hired her to work for his office. She later designed several important buildings on her own, including the Wednesday Club (1911).

In 1900 Gill designed his first large East Coast residence for Albert H. Olmsted of Newport, Rhode Island, brother of famous landscape architect Frederick Law Olmsted, Sr. The rubble-rock foundation and chimneys, shingle-clad exterior, and multi-hipped roof created a picturesque effect. Windows on the porch and sun-room could be lowered into the parapet on pleasant days.

Opposite page top: In 1902 Gill again traveled to Newport, Rhode Island, to supervise construction of a large and elaborate Spanish-style home for Miss Ellen Mason on grounds landscaped by the Olmsted firm. Gill shipped great quantities of redwood from California for use on the interiors.

Opposite page bottom: One of Gill's most daring early projects, the Moses Flower Shop in Bar Harbor, Maine (1904), featured the remarkable use of an enormous plate-glass window with unframed butted seams.

Hebbard & Gill produced many fine residences inspired
by English design. A large home for Nebraska cattleman
Bartlett Richards (1901-02) in Coronado is an impressive
example. In 1914 Walter Dupee purchased the house
and added two wings, nearly doubling its size.

Opposite page top: In 1904 Julius Wangenheim, one of
San Diego's business and cultural leaders, hired
Hebbard & Gill to design an English-style home. The use
of a recessed arched entry, rather than a covered porch,
became a trademark of Gill's later designs.
Wangenheim's collection of rare books was housed in a
handsomely outfitted library. Hazel Waterman designed
an award-winning garden for the house in 1917.

Opposite page bottom: The First Church of Christ
Scientist (1904-05) had elements of both the English and
the Mission styles, with its clinker brick walls and
buttresses and its arched windows. Constructed on a
small city lot, the church did not have a grand entrance;
instead, access was through an arcaded portico along
the east end of the structure.

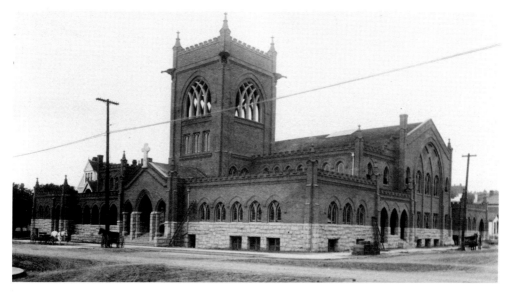

Hebbard & Gill used the English Gothic style for the First Methodist Episcopal Church (1905-07) in San Diego, one of the largest churches in the city. Controversy resulted from the architects' decision to incorporate gargoyles in the design. Several local architects—including Henry Lord Gay, Samuel G. Kennedy, and Gustavus C. Clements—defended their use in the press.

In 1905, Hebbard & Gill designed a bathhouse in La Jolla, using the tank of the former bathhouse, which had burned down. The striking linearity of their design created a handsome effect on the cliffs above La Jolla Cove.

Banker and future San Diego mayor Louis Wilde commissioned the Pickwick Theatre (1904-05), a blatant copy of the entrance to Sullivan's Transportation Building. Frank Lloyd Wright prepared designs for only three unrealized projects in San Diego. One of these was a theater façade of about this same size and date that may have been intended for the same site.

San Diego's reputation as a health resort saw the development of many facilities that catered to tubercular patients. The Rancho Guajome Health Company (1905) was proposed for a site near the mission at San Luis Rey. Hebbard & Gill designed a hotel in the Mission style for the project, which never obtained the necessary financial backing.

In 1905, Hebbard & Gill created a handsome brick and shingle residence for Charles P. Douglas (Opposite page). The arch, open terrace, and pierced parapet became familiar Gill devices. Among the house's unusual features were the unframed butted glass bay windows on the second floor and the fireplace under the stairs in the entry hall.

Originally envisioned as a half-timbered English cottage,
the exterior of the George Marston residence (1904-05)
was greatly simplified during construction. Gill carried
this modernization through to the interiors, where the
stair railing became a bold statement in verticals.

Alice Lee and her companion Katherine Teats commissioned Hebbard & Gill to design three houses around a shared garden in 1905. Miss Lee's talent for community planning had previously helped create the model town of Westport, New York, situated on property her family owned along the shores of Lake Champlain. In this, his first multiple residential design, Gill used a U-shaped pergola to connect the three houses. The low-pitched roofs, wide eaves, and strong horizontals were directly inspired by the Prairie style, and these may be the first Prairie buildings in Southern California.

In the 1890s, Rev. Frederick and Mary Cossitt had Gill design a residence and two rental cottages in Coronado. Moving to San Diego, they commissioned Hebbard & Gill to prepare drawings for a new home in 1906. Designed as a series of receding and enlarging cubic shapes with broad flat eaves, the house shows how quickly Gill adapted the Prairie style to work with his own design elements.

Several houses designed in 1906 show a combination of English and Arts and Crafts elements. The boldly geometric half-timbering of the red-brick Frederick Burnham house (above), built for George Marston's sister and brother-in-law, created a modern appearance.

A bungalow for Mrs. Ermina Carrington maintained a low profile and used English cottage detailing.

The press identified the style of the Edmund F. Parmelee house as "Cheshire," but the open terrace and pergola were familiar Gill devices.

In the George M. Hawley residence, the linear patterns of the half-timbering helped articulate the window openings and edges of the second floor.

A handsome wooden clubhouse for the San Diego
Woman's Club (1906), designed in the Arts and Crafts
style, featured projecting window boxes and stacked-
beam eaves.

Opposite page top: One of the last major projects to face
the Hebbard & Gill partnership was Germania Hall (1906-
07) for the local Concordia Turnverein. The interior
included a large auditorium, banquet hall, lodge rooms, a
ladies' parlor, a rathskeller, and a well-equipped modern
gymnasium.

Opposite page bottom: Started during the Hebbard & Gill
partnership, this hotel for Mrs. Dora Lanier was
completed by Hebbard in 1907, after the partnership had
ended. The striking horizontal design with dark bracket
eaves and recessed arcaded portico created an attractive
façade.

Beginning in 1899, Gill purchased property in the Hillcrest and Sherman Heights areas of San Diego, where he constructed a number of experimental cottages. Here he developed his techniques for flush detailing, slab doors, and thin-wall construction. Gill also had a genuine concern for people of the working class and tried to design clean, safe, and comfortable low-cost housing.

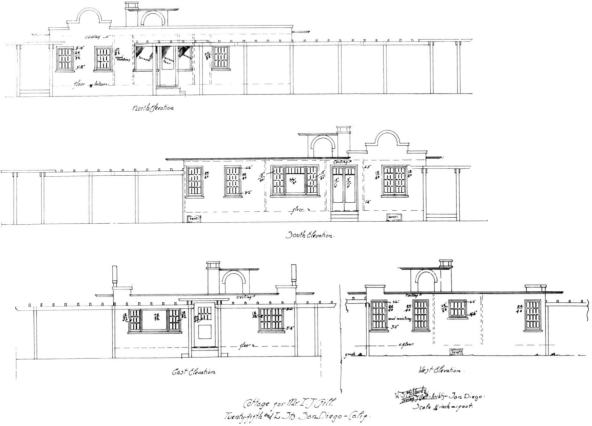

North Elevation

South Elevation

East Elevation

West Elevation

Cottage for Mr. I. J. Gill.
Twenty-fifth and L. St. San Diego - Calif.

1907: Gill & Mead

The year 1907 proved to be a critical turning point in Gill's career. After ten years, the Hebbard & Gill partnership had run its course. The end may have been hastened by a scandal involving the Dr. H. Nevill Goff residence. In April 1907, sewer inspector Joseph S. Brachman accused Gill of instructing a workman to break into the public sewer line in order to drain off standing water under the house, thereby causing debris and sand to clog the line. Denying the charges, Gill accepted full responsibility for any damage done by his workmen. An extensive and accusatory article in the April 26 *San Diego Union* must have been very damaging to the firm's reputation. By May 3, Gill began identifying himself as a partner of Frank Mead, although the dissolution of the Hebbard & Gill partnership was not officially announced until June 16.

Hebbard maintained an independent practice in San Diego until World War I. He continued using a wide variety of styles in his work, from English and Spanish to Neoclassical and Arts and Crafts. Presumably he maintained friendly relations with Gill, since Hebbard became the first president of the San Diego Architectural Association in 1910 and Gill served as secretary. During the first World War, Hebbard acted as a design consultant for military shipbuilding. After military service, he moved to Los Angeles, where he continued to practice architecture. Hebbard died at Coronado on August 24, 1930, while visiting his daughter.

Although Louis Gill claimed that the Gill & Mead partnership was "very short and not too satisfactory," there can be no denying that it had a major impact on Gill's developing style. The son of a residential contractor, Mead was born in Camden, New Jersey, in 1865. He obtained an education in architecture and opened an office with Bart Keane in Philadelphia about 1900. Early in his career, Mead took an extended trip abroad, where he sketched the architecture of Spain, North Africa, Asia Minor, Italy, and England. Adopting native dress, Mead was called "The Child of Allah" by the local inhabitants as he studied the boldly primitive forms of the indigenous architecture from Morocco to Syria. These studies led to his conviction that "A house should be an absolute expression of the soil. It should be an intrinsic part of the landscape, a harmonious note in the whole geographical song."

Sometime around 1905, Mead relocated to San Diego, where he was employed by Hebbard & Gill. When these two architects ended their association, Gill set up a partnership with Mead. Although the Gill & Mead partnership lasted only seven months, it produced three remarkable residences. Gill had already been working on plans for a large home for Melville Klauber before his partnership with Hebbard ended. Its smooth stucco walls and clean punched openings foretell much of Gill's later work. A magnificently sited beach house for Wheeler J. Bailey included designs for most of the interior furnishings, the only such project known from Gill's career. Perhaps most noteworthy of the three, the Russell C. Allen house in Bonita became Gill's first essay in totally stripped-down, anti-ornament architecture. It paved the way for his later cubistic designs.

There has been much speculation about whether Gill obtained inspiration from the Austrian architect Adolf Loos, who was waging his own war against ornament. This seems unlikely. Loos' famous essay *Ornament and Crime* (1908), which includes discussions of everything from tattoos to latrine graffiti, clearly postdates the Allen house, and other of Gill's early experiments with minimalist design. Both Gill and Loos questioned the moral, economic, and aesthetic implications of ornament, but Loos' theories were not put into

44

IRVING J. GILL, ARCHITECT

practical application until the construction of the Hugo Steiner residence (1910) in Vienna. Compared to the "bare honesty, childlike frankness, and chaste simplicity" of the Allen house, the Steiner residence looks awkward and unresolved, indicating that Loos may have been better at theory than practical application.

Although San Diego did have a large German-speaking community and Gill had a number of German clients, there is no evidence that he was aware of Loos or his writings at this time in his career. Only after Loos' essay was republished in Berlin in 1912 and Paris in 1913 did it begin to receive wide exposure. Gill did have a number of draftsmen with German surnames, but most of these were not employed until after 1907. Lloyd Wright, who did not enter Gill's office until 1912, stated that Gill had shown an interest in the work of Viennese architect Otto Wagner, but did not mention if Gill had been aware of Loos.

A comparison of Loos' essay with Gill's later writings shows clear differences between the two. For Loos, ornament was reactionary and laden with Freudian sexual overtones. He believed that "ornament is no longer a natural output of our

Top: A scandal involving the H. Nevill Goff residence (1907) may have contributed to the demise of the Hebbard & Gill partnership.

Above: The Hugo Steiner house in Vienna (1910), designed by Adolf Loos, is generally considered to be the prototype of the anti-ornament structure.

culture, and therefore represents a phenomenon of backwardness or a manifestation of degeneration." Gill, on the other hand, saw the advantage of using established regional types and chose as his model the primitive forms of the adobe missions and pueblos of the American Southwest; this model was augmented by the influence of Mead's North African studies. Writing about the missions, Gill said "in their long, low lines, graceful arcades, tile roofs, bell towers, arched doorways and walled gardens we find a most expressive medium of retaining tradition, history and romance." Such things would have been anathema to Loos.

Loos also felt that the elimination of ornament could produce a sort of social economy by simplifying the process of producing utilitarian objects. He wrote "The absence of ornament means less work and so an increase in earnings." Gill saw the economics differently, believing that money saved by the elimination of "meaningless gables, swags, machine-made garlands, fretwork and gingerbread" could be used for labor-saving devices or a better grade of materials. "If the cost of unimportant ornamentation were put into construction, then we would have a more lasting and a more dignified architecture."

Gill and Loos probably come closer in their discussions of aesthetics. By eliminating the "mask" of ornament, Loos thought that the object, rather than *representing* something, *became* the thing through the logical relationship between essential form and material. This is one of the primary concepts of abstract art. Gill wrote, "If we wish to do great and lasting work we must dare to be simple, must have the courage to fling aside every device that distracts the eye from structural beauty, must break through convention and get down to fundamental truths."

In a sense, Loos was the ultimate modernist, influenced by the most progressive artistic trends in Europe, while Gill was the ultimate revivalist, stripping established styles down to their most basic elements, and thereby making them his own. Even so, it is interesting to find numerous references to Gill as a "cubist" or "secessionist" in the press of the 1910s.

The reason Gill's partnership with Mead ended is not known. By the end of November 1907, Gill was back on his own. Mead left San Diego and traveled to Arizona, where he became outraged at the treatment of a group of Native Americans. He took the case directly to Theodore Roosevelt, who gave him authority to purchase land for the Indians. In 1909 Mead became superintendent for the Lame Deer Reservation in Wyoming and the following year returned to San Diego County, where he worked at the Pala Reservation.

In 1912 Mead formed a partnership with Richard Requa, a young architect and electrical engineer who had formerly been employed as a superintendent for Gill. Mead's interest in North African and Native American forms is evident in much of this firm's work. Mead & Requa used the Moorish arch effectively in the Webster (1913) and Sweet (1914) houses and also in the courtyard of the Palomar Apartments (1914). Hopi House (1914), a guest cottage for Wheeler J. Bailey in La Jolla, was a totally integrated Pueblo-style structure complete with exposed beams and ladders to the roof. The interiors featured authentic Indian pottery and textiles as well as a suite of furniture designed by the architects. Mead & Requa maintained their partnership until 1920, when Mead again left San Diego. He died in Santa Monica in 1940 from injuries sustained in an automobile accident.

Mead's influence on Gill should not be underestimated. Through Mead's exposure to the indigenous earth forms of North Africa and Gill's own exposure to the adobe forms of Southern California, Gill learned that simplicity was a universal language. Although his experiments were not yet over, Gill's path was clear.

The Melville Klauber house (1907-08) was a major turning point in Gill's career. Gill and others had been experimenting with the use of concrete for some time, but its plastic qualities had not as yet produced a vocabulary of its own. Although the Klauber house was frame with a stuccoed brick veneer, the smooth walls and clean-punched openings paved the way for Gill's later severe style in concrete.

The beautifully articulated interior spaces of the the
Melville Klauber house included a magnificent staircase
that formed a centerpiece up three floors, with two banks
of windows flooding the interior with light.

On the third floor, protected by the north eaves, Gill
created an artist's studio for Klauber's wife Amy, who
had studied painting with Emil Carlsen. It included a
private balcony, fireplace, and built-in seat around the
perimeter of the room.

Gill & Mead's second major project, a spectacularly sited beach house for Wheeler J. Bailey (1907) above the cliffs at La Jolla, remains one of Gill's most unusual residences. What appears to be the entrance porch actually leads to the dining room through sliding barn doors. Entrance was through the arched portico, with the front door facing the round pergola. The columns on both pergolas have been reduced to simple cylinders without capitol or base. Gill & Mead left the redwood board and batten interiors natural, with no stain, wax or varnish. A balcony surrounding the two-story living room provides access to the bedrooms. Bailey's collection of Native American rugs, baskets, and pottery complemented a suite of simple redwood furniture designed by the architects, who also painted Bailey's piano a flat Chinese red. Gill added a garage and a suite for Bailey's houseboy in 1910, and an apartment above the garage in 1932.

In August 1907 a fire destroyed the home of Russell C. Allen in Bonita. He turned to Gill & Mead to design a modern house that would be relatively fireproof. Although Gill's work had been approaching abstract simplicity for several years, in the Allen house he took the idea to new lengths. The box-like shape, clean window openings, recessed porches, and cylinder columns create a façade of classical serenity. In a signature Gill device, the glass front doors line up with glass doors on the opposite side of the house, creating a corridor of light through the center of the structure. The house was carefully positioned on its site so that the porch columns framed the best view of distant mountains. Interior woodwork had simple lines, with drop-ring pulls on built-in drawers and cabinets.

Gill continued to experiment with developing an architectural vocabulary suitable to the plastic qualities of concrete, using as his model the adobe missions and haciendas of California. The St. James Chapel in La Jolla (1907-08), Gill's most purely Mission Revival structure, captured the "hand-wrought" simplicity of this indigenous form.

Opposite page: Gill's first project after Mead's departure, a residence for Homer Laughlin, Jr. (1907), was also Gill's first building in Los Angeles. Although basically similar to the Klauber house in form, the exotic Moorish detailing shows that Mead's exposure to North African architecture had left its mark on Gill's work.

Gill designed his first "cube" house for G. W. Simmons in 1909.

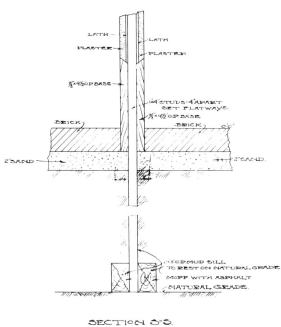

Cross-section drawing showing Gill's technique of thin-wall construction.

Classic Gill

During the five years following Frank Mead's departure from the firm, Gill continued to refine the elements that can now be identified as "Classic Gill." He still worked in a variety of styles; but when he could find sympathetic clients, Gill used the opportunity to further explore his innovative concepts of design and construction. Esther McCoy quoted Lloyd Wright as saying, "He didn't win his clients to his style by any sociological arguments, but by his great charm."

A writer for *Technical World* magazine asked Gill what he would do if a prospective client wanted him to design the best frame house he could for ten thousand dollars. Gill replied,

> "I'd first make sure of the ten thousand. Then I would use every argument I could muster to convince that person that I could build him a better and cheaper house in concrete and hollow tile than I could in wood. I might even go so far as to swear I could do a better job in concrete and tile for eight thousand than I could in wood for ten thousand, knowing he would be grateful to me in the end, even if he did not get off under twelve thousand. The point would be to make him give me a chance, and the end would justify any means."

Gill's innovations began on the interiors, where he tried to simplify housework by eliminating dust-catching ledges. As early as the Waterman house (1900), he made some of the woodwork flush with the plaster. On the third floor of the Marston house (1905) he used slab doors made up of five pieces of redwood assembled without recessed panels. Eventually he combined these features so that when a door was shut, the wall became a sheer plane, with door, frame, baseboard, and plaster all at the same level.

Next Gill tackled the bathroom, that bastion of dampness. Finding it impossible to clean under a claw-foot bathtub, Gill boxed it in and sealed it with magnesite, a lightweight material similar to concrete. He used this substance for floors, wainscot, drainboards, and sinkbacks in bathrooms and kitchens, its plastic qualities allowing it to be made "in one piece with the walls and all cornices rounded, so not a particle of grease or dirt can lodge, or dampness collect and become unwholesome."

Gill's interiors showed other concerns. Some of his houses had built-in vacuum systems that sent the dust directly to the incinerator. To prevent dirt and dust from blowing under the doors of little-used rooms, Gill raised the floor of closets and bathrooms four inches above the other floors. When possible, he installed vents in closets to allow air circulation and prevent mildew. In the Marston house, these vents became curtained six-pane windows that opened out to the broad upstairs hall where fresh air circulated from a band of large casement windows. As early as 1905, Gill had developed a technique for making ultra-thin interior walls. By using one inch by four inch studs set flatways four inches apart, he was able to make extremely sturdy walls that were only three inches thick.

Gill's innovative use of interior color frequently generated favorable comment from writers of the day. A reporter for *Architect and Engineer* wrote, "The walls are tinted a soft gray and given a surface finish (a secret of Mr. Gill's) which causes them to reflect the colors of the furnishings of each room and to echo the tenderest glory of the sky and the brilliant colors of the garden." Bertha Smith—writing for *Sunset*—observed, "At no two hours of the day are these walls alike in color, nor to the eyes of any two people. It is like living in the heart of a shell." In *The House Beautiful*, Eloise Roorbach wrote, "These white walls, as they catch the sun, present the same dazzling kaleidoscopic color seen in a field of snow, but with none of its sense of coldness or hardness. The surface becomes iridescent when the sun moves across it. The texture that makes this charm is Mr. Gill's discovery and secret."

Although Gill's clients could easily see the advantage of his interior innovations, convincing them to accept a radically different exterior took more effort. Most of Gill's first stripped-down structures were not private residences. The crisp severity of the Boys' Dormitory (1908-09) and Holly Sefton Memorial Hospital (1909) for the Children's Home Association was indicative of Gill's growing sensitivity to the power of scale and perspective. The buildings he designed for the Wilson-Acton Hotel (1908), Scripps Biological Station (1908-09), and Bishop's School (1910) in La Jolla as well as the Bishop's Day School (1909) in San Diego, reveal the monolithic monumentality of his vision.

When sympathetic clients could be found, Gill turned this vision toward domestic architecture. He wrote, "There is something very restful and satisfying to my mind in the simple cube house with creamy walls, sheer and plain, rising boldly into the sky, unrelieved by cornices or overhang of roof." Gill's first such house, designed for G. W. Simmons (1909), was a perfect cube with a small, cubic porch. Gill used this form on several occasions, sometimes adding an arched loggia to relieve the severity of the bare geometric form. It is easy to imagine how startling these houses must have looked to a generation only slightly removed from the excesses of the Victorian era. According to Louis Gill, his uncle's buildings "gave rise to such terms of derision as 'Box,' 'Soap Box Gothic,' 'Crank' and the like, but one sure way to anchor Gill in his determination was to make fun of his work."

As severe as Gill's designs were, he never expected them to stay that way. For Gill, his work was the beginning, not the end: "We should build our house simple, plain and substantial as a boulder, then leave the ornamentation of it to Nature, who will tone it with lichens, chisel it with storms, make it gracious and friendly with vines and flower shadows as she does the stone in the meadow." Even the renderings for Gill's sparest designs show that they were always envisioned with their edges softened by creepers and flowering vines. One of his favorite devices was a vine-covered pergola that acted as a direct link between structure and landscape.

Gill's interest in the relationship between architecture and nature culminated in the "garden rooms" and open courts he built into several residences, beginning with the Laughlin house (1907). In the Hamilton house (1908), a screen-covered central court enclosed on all four sides became the main room of the house complete with carpets and furniture. An arcade surrounded the court and provided the only access between rooms. Gill freely admitted that the court was borrowed from the adobe haciendas of Mexican California because "it is hard to devise a better, cozier, more convenient or practical scheme for a home."

Not everyone, however, agreed with Gill's new construction methods. In 1910 and 1911, Gill found himself in the middle of bitter battles with the city's building, plumbing, and electrical inspectors. It began with Gill wanting to use single-pipe rather than double-pipe plumbing, since this would be considerably more economical. He used this system successfully on the Tutt house in Coronado, where the codes were apparently more lenient. Gill also got into trouble when he decided to combine water and electricity in the design of the electric fountain for the plaza (now called Horton Plaza) in San Diego. Several doomsayers predicted grisly deaths by electrocution. Soon, building inspector William J. Kirkwood jumped into the fray, complaining about Gill's use of thin-wall construction in the four cube houses for Mary Cossitt on Eighth Avenue. The assistant building inspector, Henry T. Sandford, stated that the Gill studding was perfectly safe, just not up to code.

In 1910 a group of architects that included Hebbard, Gill, Samuel G. Kennedy, Charles Quayle, and Del W. Harris began to meet in an effort to assist Kirkwood in developing a new building ordinance for San Diego. Gill invited these same architects to meet at his office on August 29, 1910. Emmor B. Weaver, Richard S. Requa, and Robert Halley, Jr., also attended the gathering. Those present formed the San Diego Architectural Association, electing Hebbard president, Kennedy vice-president, Gill secretary, and Quayle treasurer.

Gill used his position as secretary of the group to become one of the most vocal opponents of the proposed ordinance because he had the most to lose. He believed that the ordinance should be written to reflect San Diego's unique situation and needs rather than merely re-writing building codes from other cities. Gill's conflict with Kirkwood became heated and the press had a field day with headlines such as "Architect Gill Raps Kirkwood" and "Kirkwood Flays Architect Gill." Finally the city council, growing weary of the quarrel, called a halt to the "rag chewing." They gave Gill a special permit to finish the Cossitt cottages but said that all future permits would have to be up to code.

Some of Gill's first structures as an independent architect show that he was exploring his quest for simplicity. The I. Isaac Irwin house (1907), begun while Gill was still in partnership with Hebbard (top), looks cluttered when compared to the Newell H. Webster house (1908). Gill used stacked-beam eaves on a number of projects at this time.

The unusual stepped parapets of the Sherwood Wheaton residence (1908) may have been Gill's attempt to disguise a pitched roof. The texture of the openwork tiles and the clinker brick foundation and chimney provided a striking contrast to the smooth stucco walls, with their crisp openings.

Opposite page top: In the Thomas Hamilton residence (1908), later owned by Mary Fulford, Gill used a boldly horizontal profile.

Opposite page bottom: The most interesting feature of the house was its screen-covered central court, which was furnished like a room and in fact served as the main room of the house. The surrounding arcade could be curtained off into additional rooms to accommodate guests.

61

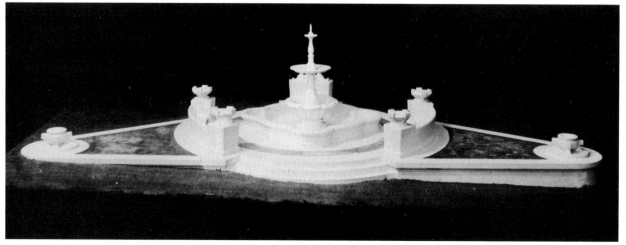

When Dr. Luke A. Port died in San Diego, his will stipulated that a sum not to exceed $11,000 be set aside to construct a memorial fountain in honor of his son Omega Port, who had been lost at sea. Port's executors commissioned Gill to design the fountain (1908), which was constructed in the Masonic section of Mt. Hope Cemetery. This photograph from Gill's files shows a model of the fountain that included decorative urns, curved benches, and glass tile mosaics. Gill's only known funerary monument, the fountain was allowed to deteriorate and was finally demolished in 1991.

One of Gill's most monolithic structures, the forty-six-room hotel designed for James Wilson and Perl Acton (1907-08) in La Jolla included a roof-top terrace with a spectacular view of the coastline. The rear elevation, which faced the ocean, created a striking geometric pattern.

As early as 1904, there had been talk of constructing a biological laboratory in the San Diego area designed by John Galen Howard, Dean of the School of Architecture at the University of California, Berkeley. In 1906 Hebbard & Gill prepared plans for a large Mission-style structure with two central courtyards. Gill's final concept, constructed in La Jolla (1908-10), was a low-cost reinforced concrete structure designed to take maximum advantage of natural lighting and ventilation. Banks of windows set in slightly recessed planes surround the building, and the interior walls have windows that can be opened to allow cross-circulation of air. Glass pavement bricks set in the floor of the upper level allow light from the skylights to filter through to the first floor. Funded by Ellen and Edward Scripps, this first structure of the now world-famous Scripps Institution of Oceanography is Gill's only building independently designated a National Historical Landmark.

The house Gill designed for Hugo Klauber (1908),
Melville Klauber's brother, had a compact geometric form
with handsome bands of casement windows. Gill
frequently placed the entrance on the side rather than
the front for added privacy.

For Peter M. Price, Gill created a low residence (1908-
09) based on the U-shaped plan of the early California
haciendas. South of the main house, Gill designed two
smaller cottages for the same client.

Gill had worked on alterations for the Children's Home Association in 1904 and 1907. In 1908 this organization asked him to prepare plans for a two-story Boys' Dormitory, followed by the Holly Sefton Memorial Hospital (above left and below) in 1909, both in reinforced concrete. These were among Gill's most progressive and beautifully scaled structures. Gill protégée Hazel Waterman later designed an Infants' Cottage (1912) and Administration Building (1924-25), which harmonized with Gill's designs.

When Annie B. Darst moved to San Diego, she began to purchase real estate. In 1908-09, she hired Gill to design a comfortable residence and two sets of apartment buildings. The house, with its handsome arch-walled garden, became one of Gill's most frequently published designs.

By 1909, the Christian Scientists had outgrown Hebbard & Gill's red brick chapel. The expanded congregation commissioned Gill to prepare plans for a new $50,000 structure in the Mission style. The original presentation sketch indicates that Gill greatly simplified his design before construction. The 900-seat auditorium, an enormous high-ceilinged volume without supporting columns, had a hidden system of truss beams that supported the span of the roof and weight of the art glass dome.

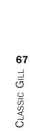

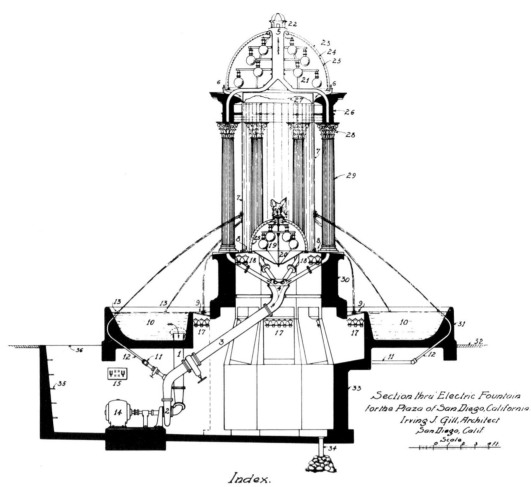

Section thru Electric Fountain
for the Plaza of San Diego, California.
Irving J. Gill, Architect
San Diego, Calif.
Scale

Index.

·1·	Suction Pipe	·21·	Upper Dome w. 48-500 Watt Tungst. Lamps
·2·	Centrifugal Pump	·22·	Bronze Lantern
·3·	Delivery Pipes	·23·	Bronze Ribs
·4·	Distributor with 7 Outlets	·24·	Bronze Grille over Glass
·5·	Bronze Overflow	·25·	Prismatic Glass
·6·	Bronze Water Catch	·26·	Marble Entablature
·7·	Circular Watersheet	·27·	Copper Ceiling
·8·	Glass Plates	·28·	Bronze Capitals
·9·	Glass Plates	·29·	8-Fluted Marble Columns
·10·	Water in Basin	·30·	Granite Base
·11·	Distributing Pipe for Side Streams	·31·	Composition Stone Basin
·12·	8-Delivery Pipes " " "	·32·	Red Tile
·13·	8-Nozels	·33·	Concrete Foundation
·14·	Electric Motor	·34·	Drain
·15·	Switch Board	·35·	Iron Steps
·16·	Flasher	·36·	Sidewalk Door
·17·	8 Light Boxes, à 15-40 Watt Tungsten Lamps with Holophane Reflectors	·37·	Water Supply
·18·	34-40 Watt Lamps with H. Reflectors	·38·	Drain of Basin
·19·	Center Dome w. 12-500 Watt Tungst. Lamps	·39·	Overflow
·20·	Reflector	·40·	Pipe to Sewer

In 1909, the San Diego Park Commission asked Gill to devise a plan to improve the appearance of the public plaza downtown, later renamed Horton Plaza. Louis Wilde offered to contribute $10,000 toward some central monument or fountain. The following year a competition was held in which Gill's design was joined by others submitted by Allen Hutchinson, Lionel Sherwood, Arthur Stibolt, and F. C. Wade. Gill's design for a Neoclassical electric fountain, styled after the Choregic Monument of Lysicrates in Athens, won the competition. Water was pumped up through the marble columns and out onto the dome—made of prismatic glass with bronze filigree—creating rainbow effects. At night, illumination came from hundreds of colored lights set on a flasher so that there were fifteen color effects, each lasting thirty seconds. A controversy arose over the safety of combining electricity and water, but the local headlines reported "Fountain is Tested; No One is Killed; It's Gill's Turn to Laugh." It was dedicated on October 15, 1910, to coincide with the opening of the U. S. Grant Hotel across the street.

When Bishop Joseph H. Johnson of Los Angeles decided to establish a preparatory school he originally planned to locate it in Sierra Madre, near Pasadena. Ellen Scripps offered to contribute a substantial sum of money to establish a school in La Jolla, and this support swayed the decision in favor of the southern community. In 1909, Gill contracted to prepare drawings for a day school in San Diego, immediately followed by the designs for the boarding school in La Jolla (1910). This became one of Gill's most important commissions and developed over a period of several years. The first two structures, Scripps Hall (opposite page top left)—a dormitory—and Bentham Hall (opposite page top right)—which contained classrooms and a small chapel—were constructed of reinforced concrete. In 1916 Carleton Winslow created a larger chapel and tower for the plan, and Gill's simple tower was removed. One of Gill's most dynamic multiple-structure plans, the design featured long arcades and broad open lawns that created an exciting interaction of indoor and outdoor spaces.

Gill could not always convince his clients to go along with his progressive designs. Several houses designed in 1909-10 seem to be a regression to his earlier work. The large number of presentation sketches for the Arthur Marston house (1909), for George Marston's son, indicate that the architect and client had difficulty agreeing on a design. Gill preferred smooth stucco, but the Marstons had always lived in brick houses. The resulting design shows typical Gill features—such as the compact shape, casement windows, and recessed arched entry—adapted to red brick.

The fortress-like entrance of the Dr. Charles L. Tutt residence (1910) in Coronado was one of Gill's most striking and unusual designs. It may indicate Gill's desire to develop something new within the brick and half-timbered idiom as previously used by Hebbard & Gill on the Richards house next door (1901-02).

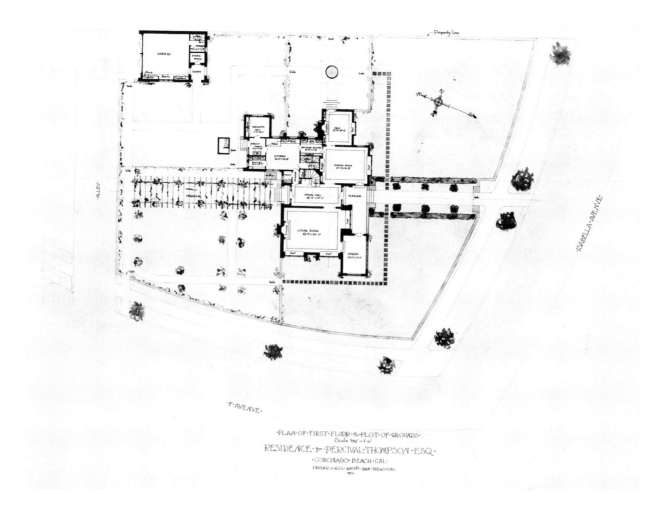

·PLAN·OF·FIRST·FLOOR·&·PLOT·OF·GROUNDS·
Scale ⅛ʺ=1'-6"
RESIDENCE·ᵒᶠ·PERCIVAL·THOMPSON·ESQ·
·CORONADO·BEACH·CAL·
IRVING·J·GILL· ARCHT· SAN· DIEGO·CAL·
1910·

Gill's sensitivity to site planning is demonstrated in his carefully conceived layout for the Percival Thompson house (1910-11) in Coronado. Gill positioned the house in such a way that the garden seat against the property line was perfectly aligned with the interior doors, which in turn were aligned with a large plate-glass window framing a magnificent view of Point Loma, allowing this vista to be enjoyed from every room on the main floor. In a perpendicular direction, the front walk, door, and hallway lined up with a pergola extending into the rear garden.

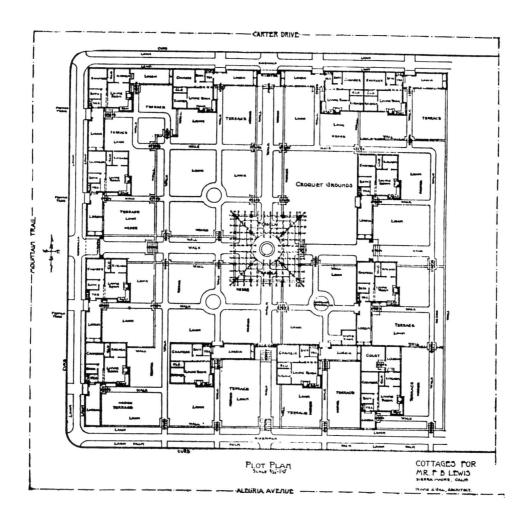

CARTER DRIVE

MOUNTAIN TRAIL

CROQUET GROUNDS

ALEGRIA AVENUE

PLOT PLAN
SCALE 3/32" = 1'-0"

COTTAGES FOR
MR. F B LEWIS
SIERRA MADRE, CALIF
IRVING J. GILL, ARCHITECT.

The Bella Vista Terrace (1910) for F. B. Lewis in Sierra
Madre was probably Gill's most famous multiple-
residential design. Using a floor plan he had tested in
some of his experimental cottages in San Diego, Gill
arranged the twelve units so that each had its own
garden plot as well as convenient access to the shared
spaces, including a large central pergola. The units on
the north and west sides were flush with the sidewalk,
and each cottage was designed so that it had a view of
the San Gabriel Valley. Although Gill intended it to be a
place for working-class families, the court proved so
popular that rents were fixed too high for them. Later, the
construction of additional units in the garden areas
ruined Gill's plan.

For Mary Cossitt, Gill designed a series of four cube houses (1910) with nearly identical floor plans. To provide variety and individual privacy to the units, he positioned them at different distances from the street and connected them with garages and arched loggias. Gill ran into trouble with the building inspector over his innovative construction methods and had to obtain a special permit to complete the structures.

RVING J. GILL. ARCHITECT

Several articles about Gill mention the story of an African-American housemaid who worked in a Gill house. She was so delighted with his labor-saving designs that she recommended Gill to the building committee of her church. The Bethel African Methodist Episcopal Church prepared a promotional brochure illustrated with beautiful line drawings by Louis Gill (1911) in order to gain support for the project. The modified Mission-style plan included a sunken garden with access to the Sunday school rooms below. The cornerstone was laid in November of 1912, with Senator Leroy Wright and Irving Gill delivering speeches at the ceremony, but it is not known how much of the plan was actually completed.

Gill's first opportunity to explore his modern design trends in a large-scale residence came in 1911 with the house he created for Henry H. Timken, of the well-known steel manufacturing family. The house and grounds took up nearly half a city block. The carefully conceived site plan and the abstract arrangement of openings show how quickly Gill's style had matured. Three loggias opened onto a screen-covered court in a free adaptation of the hacienda plan. The grounds included a large walled garden as well as a separate yard for the children.

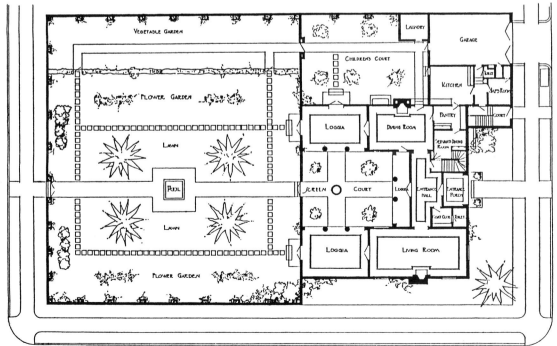

VEGETABLE GARDEN

CHILDREN'S COURT

LAUNDRY

GARAGE

FLOWER GARDEN

KITCHEN

LAWN

LOGGIA

DINING ROOM

PANTRY

SERVANTS DINING ROOM

POOL

SCREEN

COURT

LOGGIA

ENTRANCE HALL

ENTRANCE PORCH

LAWN

LOGGIA

LIVING ROOM

FLOWER GARDEN

As in all of Gill's stripped-down designs, the crisp
austerity of the Nelson E. Barker residence (1911-12)
was intended to be softened by creeping vines as the
landscaping developed. The handsome interiors included
a well-designed kitchen with magnesite countertops
coved to form a single piece with the sinkbacks.

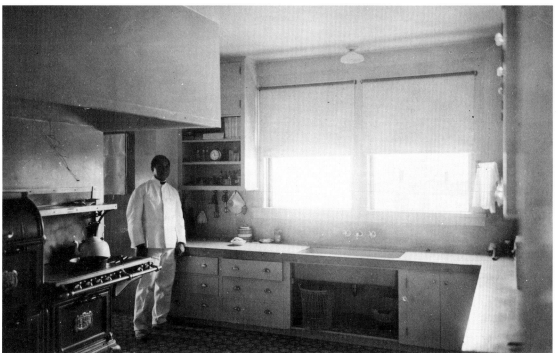

Although the Paul Miltimore house (1911) in South Pasadena is not a cube in a strict geometric sense, it exhibits a feeling of cubic monumentality. Gill carefully planned the site so as not to damage any of the existing mature live oak trees, instantly giving the house a sense of belonging. He further tied the house to its site by using parallel off-center pergolas, which act as a sort of porte-cochère over the driveway along the side. The front entrance faces a glass door leading into a sky-lit central stair hall, which in turn lines up with the glass doors off the dining room on the opposite side of the house, providing a corridor of sight and light through the center of the structure. Gill's typical flush detailing and step-up closets can be seen on the interiors. The house survives in excellent condition.

In 1912 Alice Lee and Katherine Teats hired Gill to create another multiple-residential grouping, this time surrounding a canyon site. Lloyd Wright prepared the plot plan, which shows a number of cottages with shared gardens and connecting pathways. Three structures were built along the west side in 1912 and a fourth in 1913. Louis Gill added at least one more house on the east side of the plan in 1924.

The Exposition and Los Angeles

In the summer of 1909, the San Diego Chamber of Commerce began discussing the possibility of holding a world's fair in celebration of the completion of the Panama Canal, scheduled for 1915, since the city would be the first U.S. port of call for ships passing through the canal. The idea caught on quickly, even though San Diego's population was only 39,000, making it one of the smallest cities ever to attempt such an undertaking. The Panama-California Exposition Company incorporated on September 4, 1909. In December, however, San Francisco also decided to host a fair in honor of the canal and eventually won out over San Diego for the officially sanctioned international exposition. Undeterred, San Diegans decided to proceed with their own smaller exposition.

From the beginning, the site discussed was the then largely undeveloped 1,400-acre City Park, later renamed Balboa Park for the fair. In an extensive interview published in the *San Diego Union* on November 11, 1909, Gill advocated holding the exposition along Point Loma and North Island, the two sections of land forming the entrance to San Diego Bay. He preferred this site for accessibility and convenience and also for the picturesque effects of gondolas and lights reflected on the water. Gill said "the spectacle would be one that millions of dollars could not produce in City Park." To Gill's mind, creating "unwholesome," stagnant "duck ponds" as water features in the park would be a bad idea.

In October 1910 the Building and Grounds Committee of the fair, which included former Gill clients George Marston and Russell Allen, hired the Olmsted Brothers of Brookline, Massachusetts, to be landscape designers for the fair. John C. Olmsted and Frederick Law Olmsted, Jr., operated the most prominent firm in the country that specialized in landscape architecture. Gill had designed a large home for their uncle in Rhode Island in 1900-01.

The fair directors had early decided that they wanted to use the "Spanish Mission" style of architecture, and the two architects under consideration for designing the buildings were Gill and John Galen Howard of Berkeley. Bertram Goodhue, of the prominent firm of Cram, Goodhue and Ferguson in New York, learned of the San Diego project and contacted his friend Frederick L. Olmsted, Jr., inquiring about the job. John Olmsted, who had been placed in charge of the San Diego project, cabled "No show for Goodhue."

On December 28, 1910, Goodhue wrote to Frederick Olmsted: "I can't tell you how much I am grieved by your brother's telegram, the very curtness of which lends it force. I suppose it means that they have got some incapable local talent for the job." Undeterred, that same day Goodhue also wrote to his friend Elmer Grey, a prominent Los Angeles architect: "Needless to say that I am bitterly disappointed at the turn affairs have taken and it is equally needless to ask you to regard this information as approximately confidential and not to take any hand in it unless you think the circumstances warrant you in so doing." Grey immediately began to work on Goodhue's behalf.

Goodhue's behind-the-scenes lobbying also included a letter to his "great and good friend" the Rt. Rev. Joseph H. Johnson, Bishop of Los Angeles, who Goodhue knew had a school in San Diego. In his December 28 letter to Frederick Olmsted, Goodhue stated, "I wrote the Bishop a letter after sending him a telegram. I am sure that the minute he received the telegram, he began to work for me." Obviously Goodhue did not know that Gill had designed the two Bishop's Schools in San Diego,

The Administration Building for the Panama-California Exposition in Balboa Park (1911-12).

and he was disappointed to learn that the Bishop was "devotedly attached to Mr. Irving J. Gill."

The exposition's building committee passed a resolution to negotiate with Gill. In a letter to his brother dated January 4, 1911, John Olmsted wrote "As they seemed so set on having him and as his late work pleased me pretty well and his spirit still more, I assented." Goodhue's lobbying efforts began to pay off, however, and he managed to obtain the contract. On January 30, 1911, he signed a "Memorandum of Agreement" with the exposition directors naming him "Advisory and Consulting Architect" for the fair at a salary of $12,000. This contract also called out Gill's role in the project. His salary of $7,500 indicates that Gill's contribution was to be substantial, and he was identified as "Associate" architect on the early plans for the fair. Frank P. Allen, Jr., who had previously worked with John Olmsted on the Alaska-Yukon Exposition in Seattle, had been hired as "Director of Works" on January 5. Gill enlarged the Alice Lee cottage on Seventh Avenue to accommodate Allen's family.

The site selected for the fair was the southwestern edge of the park because of its convenience to the city. As the plans became more grandiose, Allen and some of the fair directors suggested using the central mesa because it afforded more space. Goodhue also liked the idea because of its dramatic possibilities. The Olmsteds were adamantly opposed to this site, claiming that it was isolated and would cause too much damage

to the park. Political pressure for the new site grew stronger, and on August 31, 1911, the Building and Grounds Committee voted to move the exposition to the central mesa. On September 2 the Olmsted Brothers wired their resignation, stating "our professional responsibility as park designers will not permit us to assist in ruining Balboa Park." Marston also resigned from the committee, giving business and health reasons but admitting in a confidential letter to John Olmsted that it was because of the changed site, adding "...it will be a life-long regret to me that San Diego lost the services of you and your firm."

Because of Goodhue's studies of Spanish Colonial architecture and his book on the subject, this more elaborate style took precedence over the simple Mission style originally proposed. Goodhue's contract indicated that he was responsible for "the general disposition, architectural character and artistic composition of the whole." It also stated that he would be responsible for the working drawings for "either the Auditorium or Art Building," and that the drawings for whichever of these Goodhue did not design "are to be prepared by Irving J. Gill." The Art Building eventually evolved into Goodhue's California Quadrangle, the main permanent architectural feature of the fair, but the committee decided against an auditorium. Before John Olmsted's resignation, Goodhue wrote to him, "I feel that even despite the loss of the auditorium which was so lightly abandoned by everyone I will still be able, with Mr. Gill's aid, to make a very creditable effect in the permanent group."

The first building for the fair and the only one for which the architectural drawings bear Gill's name as associate architect, is the Administration Building completed in 1912. Its monolithic form, broken roofline, clean window openings, and recessed arched entry all point to Gill as the conceptual designer of this structure, and give an indication of how different the fair would have looked had Gill been named chief architect. Gill's severe designs did not conform to Goodhue's architectural plan, however. In an interview with the *Evening Tribune* on September 29, 1911, Goodhue stated "I have changed the design for the administration building in some details...the doorway, for instance, will be ornate and expressive of the general decoration of the whole group of buildings." Goodhue had his assistant, Carleton Winslow, prepare the drawings for these details, which may be why he later took credit for designing the building. This decoration was added about two years after the structure was completed, probably because the necessary artisans were not yet on site in 1912.

Gill apparently left the exposition project sometime in 1912. His name still shows up on drawings dated early in that year, but by June his name had been cut from the architects' stamp. The reason Gill left the project is not known, but several factors may have contributed to his decision. The story that he left after discovering graft in the purchasing of materials lacks support. Gill's personal philosophy, centered on building practical, lasting structures of simple beauty, was very much at odds with the whole concept of a make-believe city of temporary buildings covered with ornamentation.

In actuality, Gill's departure may have been due to a major project brewing to the north. Jared S. Torrance purchased a large tract of land south of Los Angeles from the Dominguez family in 1911. In partnership with several businessmen from Los Angeles, he formed the Dominguez Land

Company to create a model industrial town, which they named Torrance. The company hired the Olmsted Brothers, fresh from their disappointment in San Diego, to lay out the town in January of 1912. Later that month, they invited R. D. Farquhar, Elmer Grey, Sumner P. Hunt, Parker Wright, and Irving Gill to submit designs. Gill was chosen and was appointed chief architect. Certainly, designing a model industrial town was more in keeping with his practical nature than the fantasy project in San Diego.

An article in the *San Diego Union* of April 28, 1912, stated that "Since being commissioned by the Dominguez Land Company as the official architect for the industrial town of Torrance, Architect Irving J. Gill has been working overtime preparing plans for buildings to be erected there and keeping up his local work." The article went on to say that he spent Sunday to Wednesday in Los Angeles and the remainder of the week in San Diego. This must have been a difficult schedule to keep, but Gill had some talented reinforcements to assist him.

Sometime during 1911, Gill's nephew, Louis Gill, joined his office in San Diego after receiving a degree in architecture from Syracuse University. Born in Syracuse on May 9, 1885, Louis was the son of Gill's eldest brother, John D. Gill, a building contractor who had constructed several of Gill's East Coast houses. As a teenager, Louis worked with his uncle on the McCagg residence at Bar Harbor, Maine, during a summer vacation. He decided on a career in architecture, entering Syracuse University in 1907, where he studied a standard academic curriculum for the next four years.

In the spring of 1912, Frank "Lloyd" Wright, Jr., another promising designer, joined Gill's office. Lloyd Wright and his brother John had come to San Diego as draftsmen for the Olmsted Brothers. After the Olmsteds' departure, John went to work for a local building company before entering the office of Harrison Albright, where he designed the Golden West Hotel (1913). Sculptor Alfonso

Iannelli, who later created the sculptures for the famous Midway Gardens in Chicago, produced the modernistic decorative figures on the corners of the hotel. Iannelli and Gill collaborated on the design of a tower project for Mission Beach which must date to this period. This may have been for John D. Spreckels, who was developing attractions in Mission Beach and also owned the Golden West.

Lloyd Wright later stated that he had admired Gill's buildings before he discovered who had designed them. He did not know until much later that Gill and his father had once been co-workers. Lloyd entered Gill's office and worked on several important projects, including the canyon houses for Misses Lee and Teats, the barracks for the Riverside Portland Cement Company, and the Barker house, among others. When Irving Gill established his office in Los Angeles late in 1912, he took Lloyd Wright with him and left the San Diego office in the hands of Louis Gill. Wright remained with Irving Gill until 1915.

Sometime about 1912, Gill purchased some equipment used in concrete "tilt-slab" construction. The process had been developed by Col. Aiken of the U.S. Army and used in the Philippines for constructing barracks during the Spanish-American War. Walls of hollow tile and reinforced concrete, complete with door and window frames, could be cast on a horizontal "table," and then slowly tilted into position by means of a single engine. Having trouble finding contractors for this unusual system, Gill eventually formed the Concrete Building and Investment Company and became his own contractor. He first used the process in constructing the Mary Banning house (1913-14) in Los Angeles. Later, he built the La Jolla Woman's Club (1913-14) and the La Jolla Community Center (1914-16) using the same method.

The middle of this decade found Gill at the peak of his career. Between 1913 and 1916, he created three acknowledged masterworks: the La Jolla Woman's Club, the Ellen Scripps residence in La Jolla, and the Walter Dodge house in West

The buildings for the Panama-California Exposition of 1915 helped popularize the Spanish Colonial styles of architecture.

Equipment used in the tilt-slab construction of the La Jolla Woman's Club (1913-14).

Hollywood. Gill received wide exposure through articles in magazines such as *Architect and Engineer, Architectural Record, Craftsman, House and Garden, House Beautiful, Sunset* and *Vogue*. It is significant that Gill's work turns up frequently in the pages of Gustav Stickley's *Craftsman* magazine. Perhaps more than any other American architect, Gill embodied Stickley's ideals of practicality and honesty of design, as well as the qualities of simplicity and sound workmanship that marked Stickley's furniture designs.

George Wharton James, who had been associate editor of *Craftsman* magazine, singled Gill out for praise in a chapter on "California's Domestic Architecture" in his book *California, Romantic and Beautiful* (1914). Discussing Gill, James wrote:

Early impressed by the wonderful adaptability of the architecture of the Missions to the climate and scenic environment of California he sought, not as so many architects have done, to imitate or follow after in their work, but to absorb from the original sources of their inspiration. There is all the difference in the world between more or less slavish copying, even though genius may aid one to modify with pleasing effect, and gaining the original inspiration and allowing it to work out in its own new way, as, in the Missions it then worked.

After reading James' praise of Gill, Los Angeles architect Elmer Grey, who had lobbied to help Goodhue obtain the contract for the San Diego fair, fired off a long and irate letter to James on December 16, 1914. Grey called Gill's work "unrefined," and wrote "as one who has himself given some study to California architecture, and whose critical opinions have been regarded highly by leading magazine editors, I can not refrain from entering a private word of protest." Grey sent a copy of his letter to Goodhue, who replied, "As for Gill, while I don't, by any means, coincide with all his views, and not at all with his theory that ornament is unnecessary, I do think that he has produced some of the most thoughtful work done in the California of today, and that for the average architect, his theories are far safer to follow than mine, or even perhaps yours."

In his response, Grey told Goodhue that he was not converted. "I think more of your architecture than I do of your critical opinions—some of the latter of which are punk! I was not nettled at the 'praise given another' but at that given a dangerous kind of work. I think Gill's work is apt to do harm, not in itself, because the majority of people will form their own opinion of it, but through its evoking the admiration of such influential chaps as George Wharton James and Bertram Grosvenor Goodhue!"

Gill's popularity, however, had already reached its peak. For the May 1916 issue of *Craftsman*, Gill wrote an extensive article titled "The New Architecture of the West," in which he expounded on his progressive ideas about architecture. Ironically, 1916 also marked the bankruptcy of Stickley's Craftsman empire and the beginning of the end of Gill's popularity. Although several significant projects were still ahead, the last twenty years of Gill's life saw the completion of less than 10 percent of his total output.

No doubt a number of factors contributed to Gill's decline in popularity. The introduction of the decorative Spanish Colonial style of architecture at the San Diego fair started a trend away from Gill's austere simplicity. Immediately after the fair, World War I put a damper on most building activities. In the decade that followed the war, the newly affluent wanted their wealth to show, and Gill's simple designs, no matter how well built, were not as visually impressive as the showy "Spanish-style" palaces being constructed throughout Southern California. Those preferring modern design often turned to the more decorative Art Deco style. During the Prohibition era of the 1920s, San Diego found itself to be a gateway to the liquor and gambling available in Mexico, just across the border, and began to consciously adopt an artificial Spanish-Mexican look, with all its romantic imagery.

After initially leaving the San Diego office in his nephew's hands, Irving Gill took Louis Gill on as a partner late in 1914. During their five-year partnership, both seem to have worked on independent projects as well. In 1916, Gill & Gill completed the La Jolla Community Center and Gilman Hall for the Bishop's School, and they also developed plans for a large hospital for San Diego that was never built. That same year, Louis Gill designed a comfortable home for Harry Wegeforth, founder of the San Diego Zoo, and later produced designs for the zoo itself, including an enormous flight cage and zoo hospital, both funded by Ellen Scripps. The last known projects of the Gill & Gill partnership are a duplex for Louis Wilde in Coronado (1919) and a Catholic church in Coronado (1919-20), the working drawings for which were completed by Louis Gill after the partnership ended.

Louis Gill went on to become a prominent and highly respected architect. He designed a number of significant churches, hospitals, private residences, and public buildings. The John W. Mitchell Art Gallery in Coronado was one of his favorite and most unusual projects, sadly demolished after the death of Mrs. Mitchell in 1931. In 1935 Louis Gill became the chairman of the group of four architects chosen to design the new San Diego City-County Administration Building, working with William Templeton Johnson, Richard S. Requa, and Samuel W. Hamill. The younger Gill served on numerous local, state, and national architectural boards and was named a Fellow of the American Institute of Architects in 1942. Retiring in 1955, Louis Gill died on August 19, 1969, in Studio City, California, where he had moved to be closer to his children.

Few projects are known from Irving Gill's hand in the years around 1920. Some residences and apartment complexes in the Los Angeles area could not have kept him very busy. Without adequate opportunity to use the tilt-slab construction method, Gill's Concrete Building and Investment Company turned into a financial disaster. The commission for a large home for Chauncey Dwight Clarke in Santa Fe Springs (1920-22) must have helped ease his financial situation, but this proved to be Gill's last major residence.

In November 1922 Gill found himself in the office of Horatio Warren Bishop, supervising architect for the Carthay Center project in Los Angeles, looking for a job as a draftsman. Earlier that year, a syndicate of Los Angeles businessmen had acquired the land lying south of Wilshire Boulevard between Fairfax Avenue and Beverly Hills. Besides residences, the tract was to include a business/shopping center, school, chapel, and theater. To ensure uniform quality in the development, the promoters offered architectural services at no additional cost to purchasers of lots.

Bishop later recorded his first impression of Gill. "His mode of dressing was unusual; a long tan smock, tan leather puttees and black shoes. He wore no hat and his heavy shock of black hair and ruddy face left no doubt that he was a man of the arts." Before hiring Gill, Bishop asked to see some of his work. Gill took him on a tour of the Laughlin house, the Horatio West apartments, and the Dodge house, ending in a visit with architect R. M. Schindler and his wife in their new home nearby. Impressed by what he had seen, Bishop hired Gill on a trial basis at a salary higher than the other draftsmen.

Gill worked on six houses for the Carthay Center project. Some of these were in the English style, but Gill was given the freedom to design in his own unique style as well. Unfortunately, Gill's trial period did not end happily. According to Bishop, Gill disrupted several client meetings, trying to persuade the buyers to go with his more progressive ideas. Approaching one of the syndicate owners, Gill even tried to have himself named supervising architect instead of Bishop. Gill was let go in January 1923, after only two months of employment.

The next few years must have been difficult ones for Gill. In 1924 he completed his last known single-family residence, a modest home for Arthur J. Misner in the city of Bell. A store and apartment building for W. I. Castanien in Los Angeles (1924) is the only other project known from the mid 1920s. Gill's life at this time may also have been complicated by failing health. When he died in 1936, his death certificate records that he had suffered a heart attack in 1924. A sketch for an unidentified apartment building dated 1925 indicates that he was not completely idle during his recovery, but no additional Gill projects are recorded until 1927.

El Roi Tan Hotel and office building.

In 1912, Gill received the commission to design a number of commercial and residential structures for the model industrial town of Torrance southwest of Los Angeles. Gill's work included hotels, office and industrial buildings, workers' housing, a two-room school house, and a railroad bridge and depot. The Y-shaped plan was laid out by the Olmsted Brothers, who oriented its central axis to give a distant view of Mt. San Antonio, directly above Gill's railroad station. The industrial areas were positioned so that the prevailing winds would carry smoke away from the residential neighborhoods, and Gill made a special effort to provide the manufacturing structures with adequate light and ventilation. An article in the March 1913 issue of *Sunset* magazine contrasted Torrance with the workers' tenements of London and New York, stating that "the well-being of the worker has at last been clearly recognized as the source of the largest, most permanent profit." Still, not all workers were pleased. Gill's simple designs eliminated the need for many specialized building skills, and his monastically severe cottages proved difficult to rent.

Torrance School.

Rubbercraft Corporation building.

In 1911 Gill completed a house for C. L. Gorham across
from Balboa Park. The use of stacked-beam eaves
reflects the Arts and Crafts style (the angelic apparition
on the roof is actually part of the church in the next
block). The broad bands of casement windows and a
recessed arched entry are typical of Gill's work during
this period; these features also turn up below in the
Frank J. Belcher, Jr., residence (1912).

When George Kautz learned that the La Jolla Woman's Club—soon to be erected adjacent to his property—was to be in a new style of architecture, he decided to use the same architect in order to harmonize the style of the two buildings. Most of the drawings for the Kautz house (1913) were done by Louis Gill, in typical Irving Gill style. The use of creeping vines to soften the edges is clearly apparent in this early view. Interior features include a fireplace with a tile hearth and an etched copper motto reading "God's Providence Is Mine Inheritance." John Philip Sousa and his family later occupied the house for a time.

In 1912, Gill began working on plans for a clubhouse for the La Jolla Woman's Club which was funded by Ellen Scripps. A masterpiece of understatement, the building disappears behind a screen of pergolas and arcades. Gill's skill as a site planner created an easy flow between garden, arcade, and interior. December of 1913 saw the laying of the cornerstone, and the walls were constructed by the tilt-slab method early the following year. The club held its first meeting in the new building on October 5, 1914. Louis Gill made some alterations in 1922 and again in 1926, including the enlargement of the lunchroom and the addition of decorative ironwork around the entrance. It remains one of Gill's finest structures.

Having a longstanding interest in low-income and workers' housing, Gill asked the Riverside Portland Cement Company to let him design barracks for its migrant workers (1913). As envisioned by Gill, the complex would have included two rectangular structures surrounded by trees with central courtyards, as seen in this rendering by Lloyd Wright. Gill intended to use the tilt-slab construction method, creating a continuous outside wall and a central garden. Apparently, Gill was unable to convince the company to go along with his full concept. The complex was finally constructed of wood but did have the amenities of a central garden with a covered pavilion.

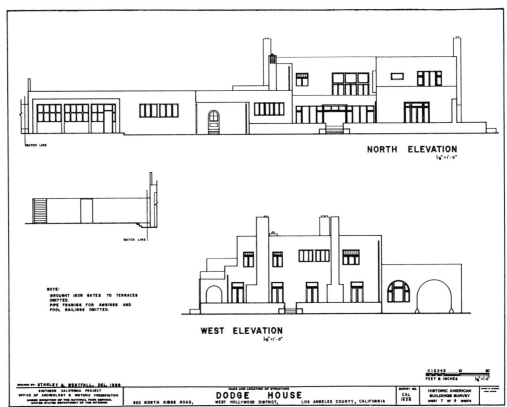

NORTH ELEVATION

WEST ELEVATION

NOTE:
WROUGHT IRON GATES TO TERRACES
OMITTED.
PIPE FRAMING FOR AWNINGS AND
POOL RAILINGS OMITTED.

DODGE HOUSE

In 1914, Gill began work on a large home for Walter Dodge in West Hollywood that came to be acknowledged as his residential masterpiece. Unlike his usual compact designs, this project's generous site allowed Gill to create a floor plan that sprawled around courts and terraces. The front elevation featured a broadly arched porte-cochère, while the abstract arrangement of window openings and cubic shapes of the rear elevation demonstrated Gill's mastery of form, proportion, and scale. Because of the extensive detailing, including sheer interior walls of carefully matched Honduras mahogany, the house was not completed until 1916.

During the summer of 1915, La Jolla residents were
terrorized by a series of unexplained fires. On the
evening of August 7, fires were set in Gill's St. James
Chapel, the cottage of Miss Virginia Scripps, and the
home of Ellen Browning Scripps, which was destroyed.
Ellen Scripps had employed Gill on several projects for
her estate and had funded other buildings of his design
in La Jolla. No doubt she also appreciated his interest in
fireproof construction and immediately hired him to draw
up plans for a new residence. The Scripps house (1915-
16) was another of Gill's great works, similar in concept
to the Dodge house but more compact. Two antique
pergolas, all that remained of the older structure, were
incorporated in Gill's design. Like two outstretched arms,
they connected to a central covered porch from which the
house grew in cubic simplicity. The rear elevation had
large windows to allow maximum enjoyment of the ocean
view. As in the Dodge house, the interiors featured
beautifully matched flush panels of Honduras mahogany.

In 1914 Ellen Scripps provided funding for a public playground, community house, and director's cottage (1914-16). Gill & Gill drew up the plans, and the main structure was constructed by the tilt-slab method. With the completion of the Scripps house across the street, the central area of La Jolla began to take on a unique architectural identity. In close proximity were several other major buildings by Gill: the St. James Chapel, the Bishop's School, the Kautz house, and the La Jolla Woman's Club.

Gilman Hall (1916) for the Bishop's School was Gill's last major building in La Jolla, done in partnership with Louis Gill. Its arcades featured openings to let in light while still affording protection during inclement weather.

During the mid 1910s, Gill prepared drawings for several apartment projects for Homer Laughlin, Jr., none of which was apparently ever constructed. For the same client, Gill designed the Laughlin Theatre Building (1914-15) in Long Beach, a large structure that included store fronts, offices, and a motion picture auditorium. Some of its details show a Moorish influence. Built of steel, concrete, and brick, it survived the disastrous Long Beach earthquake of 1933, but has since been demolished.

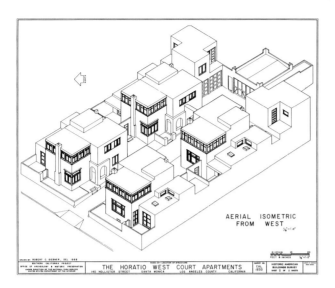

One of Gill's last multiple housing projects, the Horatio West Court (1919) in Santa Monica, was constructed of reinforced concrete. Because the site was close to the ocean, Gill developed a special moisture barrier inside the walls. Each unit had a separate entrance and private courtyard, as well as a view of the ocean and mountains from the second floor. Architect Richard Neutra, intrigued by the novel construction method, published a description of the project in his book *New Building in the World* (Vienna, 1930).

In 1919 Louis Wilde, now mayor of San Diego, commissioned Gill & Gill to design a duplex for a triangular lot he owned in Coronado. Gill claimed that it was the first apartment house in Southern California to be equipped entirely with electrical appliances: hot-air circulating floor heaters, in-line water heaters, and built-in electrical ranges in the kitchens. The design included a garage for each unit and a screened court.

IRVING J. GILL, ARCHITECT

The last known project of the Gill & Gill partnership is
Sacred Heart Church in Coronado (1919-20). The project
was initially designed by Irving Gill, and Louis Gill
prepared the working drawings after the partnership
ended. A Moorish influence can be detected in the
smooth walls, skillfully broken by cubic projections with
carefully placed openings, which create an interesting
play of light.

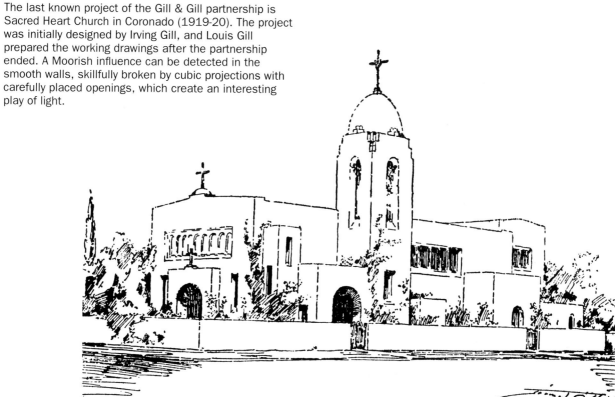

Gill's last major residential design was an 8,000-square-foot structure built on a sixty-acre citrus grove in Santa Fe Springs. The Chauncey Dwight Clarke house (1920-21) was constructed by the "Gill System" of poured-in-place reinforced concrete, for which Gill had made a patent application. From the arched porte-cochère, one enters a "fern room" which opens onto a two-story central courtyard. This court has simple columns on three sides, supporting the upper rooms and balconies. The court included a projection area from which silent movies could be shown. An unusual design feature is the use of leaf patterns cast into the wall surfaces. It is the only one of Gill's large residences in his classic style that survives in near-original condition.

IRVING J. GILL, ARCHITECT

A one-story home for Arthur J. Misner (1924) in the city of Bell, near Los Angeles, is Gill's last known single family residence. Constructed around an inner court, the house also featured typical Gill arched entry and projecting window boxes. The tile coping around the roofline is a later addition.

Final Years

Although there are no Gill buildings known from 1925 or 1926, his situation began to improve in the late 1920s. He obtained the commission to prepare plans for the First Church of Christ Scientist of Coronado in 1927. A modest structure in typical Gill style, it demonstrates that he had lost none of his skill as a designer.

Another significant event in Gill's life took place in the late 1920s. At the age of fifty-eight, he decided to marry. Information about his wife, Marion Waugh Brashears, is limited and frequently conflicting. The daughter of Canadians Charles J. and Jean (Ross) Waugh, she was born in Illinois on May 31, 1870, and was the same age as Gill. Several sources identify her as the niece of John Charles Shaffer of Chicago, the multi-millionaire president of syndicates that owned several newspapers and streetcar systems in the Midwest.

Marion moved to Southern California in 1917, perhaps after the death of her first husband. She must have met Gill soon after her arrival: an announcement of their wedding in the *San Diego Union* states that their marriage was the culmination of a ten-year romance. The wedding took place on May 28, 1928, at the bride's home in Palos Verdes Estates, an exclusive residential community near Los Angeles that had been designed by the Olmsted Brothers. The bride, a teacher and vocational analyst, was identified as a "woman of affairs" who served as treasurer and parliamentarian for the Palos Verdes Women's Club.

Although Gill had always been popular with women, no previous romantic involvements are known. His grandnephew, Rev. John Gill, later said, "I think he finally married simply because he wanted company in his old age." Gill moved in with his wife at Palos Verdes, but this arrangement was short-lived. His health began to fail, and the doctors advised him to relocate to an avocado ranch his wife owned at Carlsbad, just north of San Diego. He made the move in March 1929.

Soon after returning to San Diego County, Gill associated briefly with John Selmar Siebert in the preparation of designs for a modern schoolhouse for the South Bay Union School District. Born in Fürstenwalde, Prussia, on September 28, 1864, Siebert was the son of American citizens who had returned to their homeland for a visit. After being graduated from Lehigh University in 1886 with a degree in civil engineering, he later studied architecture and opened a practice in the early 1890s. Moving to San Diego in 1909, Siebert specialized in non-residential architecture. Having a strong interest in education, he designed a number of schools and won election to the Board of Education in 1929, the same year he succeeded to the presidency of the San Diego Architectural Association.

As Siebert's associate, Gill prepared at least four presentation drawings for a school. Siebert's role in this project appears to have been minimal and may simply have been to provide security for the clients should Gill's health prevent his completion of the project. The final design was published in the *San Diego Union* on October 20, 1929. Unfortunately, the stock market crash and resulting depression prevented construction. Siebert went on to become a member of the San Diego City Council in 1935, where he helped write a uniform building code for the city. He also became a member of the Civic Center Building Committee in 1936. Sometimes referred to as the "dean" of San Diego architects, he died in 1948.

In 1929 Gill started work on the final major project of his career, a group of civic buildings for the city of Oceanside. Initially, he designed a civic center that was to cover an entire city block. The buildings were to be placed around the edges of the

Irving Gill worked with John Siebert on the design of an elementary school for the South Bay Union School District in 1929.

site, surrounding decorative gardens in the center. Unfortunately, the economic depression of the 1930s prevented the realization of the full plan. A fire and police station (1929-31) and a building used as the city hall (1934) were the only two Gill structures completed. Two schools of Gill's design were also built in Oceanside (1930-31), but plans for a recreation palace, an auditorium, and a public swimming pool went unrealized.

In the early 1930s, Gill kept himself busy with plans for a number of small projects, most of which were never built. He designed several commercial structures as well as a "Spanish Village" for Carlsbad. In 1932 former client Wheeler J. Bailey had Gill add an apartment above his garage and also prepare plans for another cottage on the site that did not get constructed.

Gill's last significant commission came in 1932. In that year he obtained the contract to design twelve cottages and a small church for the newly established Rancho Barona Indian Reservation near Lakeside. Named after Padre Josef Barona, who served at the Mission San Diego de Alcalá from 1798 to 1810, Rancho Barona was purchased by the federal government as a

resettlement for a group of Indians being displaced by the construction of a dam and reservoir at El Capitan. The government had Gill create a cottage for each of the twelve original families, its size depending on the number of children. He lived on the site to supervise construction, and some of the older tribal members recall how he taught them to use bent spoons to create the cove between the concrete floor and walls. Gill took a group of them to see his work in La Jolla and also to look at fabrics he thought would be appropriate for the interiors, indicating his personal concern for clients of all economic levels. Although the cottages were federally funded, the Indians themselves paid for the construction of the church.

In the last year of Gill's life, he may have tried to become involved in the various federal work programs established during the Depression era to keep people employed. Several local architects, including Gill, prepared sketches for a Veteran's Memorial building for San Diego that seems to have been a government competition. Probably through former associates Louis Gill and John Siebert, Irving Gill also prepared a design for a "Glazed Tower" for the new San Diego City-

Gill's architectural innovations had a strong influence on local building companies, as can be seen in this house constructed by Southern California Home Builders (1914).

County Administration Building, another project funded by the Works Progress Administration.

Gill died in San Diego on October 7, 1936. Ironically, his death certificate listed his occupation as "laborer." According to family members, Gill's wife dabbled in assorted forms of oriental mysticism and belonged to the Science of the Mind Church. When Louis Gill went to visit him during his final illness, Gill instructed his nephew that, in order to humor his wife, he was to be buried in a shroud rather than a casket. In fact, Gill's body was cremated and the ashes released to his wife. Their final disposition is not recorded. Marion Gill survived until her own death in Los Angeles on December 1, 1952.

Just before his death, Gill was working on plans for the Zara Witkin theater in Hollywood. His final building, completed after he died, was a structure for the *Blade-Tribune* newspaper in Oceanside. According to obituaries published in *Southwest Builder and Contractor* and *Architect and Engineer*, "At the time of his death authorities from Vienna were in this country collecting material with the idea of publishing a monograph of his work." Such a book was never completed.

Trying to establish an impression of Gill the man is not easy. Almost nothing survives in the way of personal papers or correspondence. In October 1958, on the occasion of an exhibit of the architect's work that took place in Los Angeles, Louis Gill drafted a speech that discussed his uncle's life and work. The following quotations are taken from those notes.

Irving Gill was a very good looking man, of medium build. He had a wonderfully slightly curly head of dark hair, which remained with him until his death. Another asset was his beautiful speaking voice, which he used very effectively. In all the years I seldom saw him angry, but he loved to argue. He was not a university trained architect but his self-administered culture made him an interesting talker.

He was never entirely satisfied with any design and he destroyed many drawings. He never kept any sort of record of his achievements and was never concerned much with money.

To my mind Irving Gill was much more than a pioneer architect in California. He was an innovator, constantly devising new ideas, not only in exterior design, but in hundreds of details, always considering such fundamental things as costs and

Hazel Waterman, who had worked for Gill on a number of projects, designed the Wednesday Club in 1911. The smooth walls, recessed entry, and broad open terrace flanked by matching pergolas are all classic Gill devices. Ernest Batchelder provided four decorative tile panels for the façade, and Anna Valentien made the etched copper nameplate, door hardware, and the pierced brass and art glass lantern that hung from a bracket on the porch.

materials and methods of construction, and always abhorring anything done for show. An indefatigable worker, never satisfied and quite willing to sacrifice anything to his art. In fact, to me, he seemed obsessed with the idea.

Gill's impact on the architectural development of San Diego was profound. His associations, through partnership or as an employer, included nearly every significant architect who worked in San Diego during the first four decades of this century. Many of the home building companies at this time adopted his design features, often employing draftsmen who had previously worked for Gill. Although few of these designers were willing to sacrifice as much as Gill did in his quest for simplicity, many of his innovative ideas turn up in their work. In fact, some of their buildings have been erroneously attributed to Gill over the years.

The ten-year partnership with Hebbard certainly influenced Gill's development, but Hebbard also gained from his exposure to Gill. Hebbard's Charles Fox house (1908) and Harry Gregg residence (1909) show the Gill preference for smooth surfaces and clean lines. Louis Gill spent the early part of his career working in his uncle's style, as seen in the Harry Wegeforth house (1916), but even later projects such as the Mission Hills Congregational Church (1920) continue a strong Gill influence.

Hazel Waterman did drafting for Gill on various projects from about 1905 to 1907. Some of her later independent work—particularly the Wednesday Club (1911), and the Infant's Cottage

The Charles L. Hyde residence (1912) in the Loma Portal area of San Diego was designed by John B. Stannard and Eugene M. Layman. The stacked-beam eaves and recessed entry with projecting porch above were typical Gill devices. Layman had previously worked as a draftsman for Gill on a number of projects that used these design elements, including the Annie Darst house (1908-09), which this structure closely resembles.

(1912) and Administration Building (1924-25) for the Children's Home Association—is very much influenced by Gill's style. Although Emmor Brook Weaver only worked in Gill's office for a short time, Weaver's masterly use of redwood may have been inspired by Gill's fondness for this material. Weaver's Stella Rucker house (1911), formerly attributed to Gill because of its smooth walls and clean arched openings, features a handsomely hand-finished redwood interior.

After working as superintendent for Gill, Richard Requa started his own practice about 1911. The residence he designed for John S. Hawley that year has many of Gill's classic features and for many years was attributed to Gill (as the "Chase" house). In 1912 Requa became the partner of Frank Mead. One of their earliest projects, a low, Gill-like residence for Frederick Webb (1913), is arranged around a central court in typical Gill fashion. When Mead left San Diego in 1920, Requa took Herbert Jackson, who had also worked as a draftsman and superintendent for Gill, to be his partner. In the 1920s, Requa & Jackson helped popularize the style known as "California Architecture," which clearly had its roots in Gill's designs, with the addition of more romantic Mediterranean detailing.

A number of lesser-known architects had also worked in Gill's office. The names of Adolph Beyer, Charles Kruegal, Eugene M. Layman, J. B. Lyman, Jr., Albert O. Treganza, Harry Vaughn, and Albert Walker, among others, can be found as draftsmen on plans from Gill's office. Each went on to become an independent architect, no doubt bringing some of Gill's ideas to their work. Other Gill associates, including Lloyd Wright and Horatio Warren

Del W. Harris experimented with Gill's style in several structures. His People's National Bank in National City (1911) shows the cubic monumentality and clean arched openings preferred by Gill.

Bishop, acknowledged with appreciation their debt to his innovative designs, and Del W. Harris, who had no direct association with Gill, showed his admiration by designing several buildings—including the People's National Bank in National City (1911) and the Moson Block in Coronado (1911)—in Gill's classic style.

Trying to determine Gill's influence outside Southern California is more difficult. Although there was broad interest in his work through references to it in national publications, Gill's flat-roofed designs without protective eaves would only have been practical in the more arid parts of the country. The Ronada Court (constructed in Berkeley in the 1910s), if not actually designed by Gill, was certainly inspired by his Lewis Court in Sierra Madre, with its repeated floor plans, loggias, and shared gardens. Gill-inspired projects in other parts of the country have not yet been identified.

The Streamline Moderne style that flourished in the 1930s, with its clean geometric forms, crisp edges, and smooth surfaces, shows that Gill may simply have been twenty years ahead of his time. The November 1931 *Architectural Record* published photographs and plans for the model of a very Gill-like "cube" house designed by architect and industrial designer Joseph Urban. Like so many pioneers, Gill's true significance as one of the few architects to develop an original and highly individual style of architecture has only recently come to be widely recognized. This makes the destruction of so many of his important designs all the more regrettable. It also challenges present and future generations to preserve that which remains.

In 1927 Gill obtained the commission to design a small
structure for the First Church of Christ Scientist of
Coronado. Planned around an open courtyard that is
deeply set back from the street, the church was placed
at the rear of the lot. An arcade connected it to a
separate reading room at the corner of the lot. The
arcade in front of the church has openings that allow
light to enter the tall arched windows. The beautifully
scaled and carefully assembled cubic forms show that
Gill had gained in sensitivity without losing any of his
power. One of Gill's most exquisitely proportioned
structures, it survives in excellent condition.

Gill's master plan for the Oceanside Civic Center (1929) shows a complex designed to cover an entire city block with central gardens and fountains. Due to economic conditions during the Depression, only the fire and police station (1929-31, left corner), and a small structure used as the city hall (1934, far corner), were ever constructed. The fire and police station, with its hose tower and narrow arched windows, featured an engine room, offices, and court house on the first floor, and a dormitory, club room, kitchen, locker room, and jails above. Gill designed both the men's and the women's jails to have open skylights with steel-bar grates.

Gill also prepared plans for two schools in Oceanside. The first design (below), identified as "Moorish" in the local press, was for the Americanization School (1930-31) where foreign students, mostly Mexicans, could be taught English before becoming citizens. The domed entrance structure connected to three staggered classrooms, with walls of glass facing a recreation area. A two-room kindergarten (above) with a bell tower (1931), constructed in an L-shaped plan, had an open court surrounded by an arcade.

In the Assumption of the Blessed Virgin Mary Church (1932-34) for the Indians of the Rancho Barona reservation near Lakeside, Gill went full circle back to his original inspiration. Built of cement brick made on site, the diminutive Mission-style structure featured stepped buttresses and a bell tower. The entrance was originally at the side, but this was later changed to the front. At the same time, a second bell tower was also added to Gill's design, creating a more symmetrical façade.

Gill's *Blade-Tribune* building in Oceanside (1936), completed after his death, provides an indication of how his style could have been assimilated into the 1930s style known as Streamline Moderne. All the details were cast in place when the concrete was poured.

"New Ideas About Concrete Floors"

by Irving J. Gill.

Reprinted from *Sunset* Magazine, December 1915.

Why do most people hate concrete floors? Partly because we are all slaves to habit, partly because concrete floors are not what they really ought to be.

Twenty years ago I built for myself a concrete floor. I expected it to be cold, I expected it to be damp, I expected it to be all the uncomfortable things people said it would be. I found it warm and dry and all the comfortable things people had not said it would be. Best of all, I knew it would never harbor the vermin of sorts that infest old wooden flooring, mice that scamper at night, or the accidental cat.

The charges against the concrete floor are precisely those made years ago against the cement sidewalk. We had come from dirt paths where feet find comfort in the happy medium between dust and mud, and the board sidewalk with its awkward surprises of heel-trapping cracks, loose nails and broken boards, to the smooth, hard, level cement. At first the rut-lovers wailed. But who would now go back to uneven board walks or the pleasant uncertain earth paths? In foreign lands where the cement walk is unknown, who does not pray long and loud for its revelation to all the world?

Perhaps the earth floor is the ideal thing, but we have passed that stage, and in the evolution of house-building the wood floor is finding a rival. Wood floors above ground without a basement are unhealthful. There is always a musty odor from the poisonous fungus growing on the wood and on the ground. The ground underneath an old house is poisoned to such an extent that plants will not grow in it. The soil from under a cement sidewalk is very fertile.

Most concrete floors have not yet been developed beyond the sidewalk stage. If half the thought and time and money had been expended on perfecting the concrete floor that has been spent on developing wood from the rough board sidewalk to fine parquetry flooring, everybody would want the concrete.

To overcome the popular prejudice against concrete floors is the business of the architect. There are certain definite conditions to be observed in the laying of concrete floors. They are fundamental and in their strict observance lies the answer to the charge of the physical discomfort of concrete. After practical objections are overcome, attention may be given to esthetic considerations.

Concrete floors are usually laid free from the ground, with a dead air space underneath. In most of my houses the concrete floors are laid directly on the ground, doing away with air circulation under the floor and giving a more equable temperature. They are raised at least twenty-one inches above the surrounding ground, and particular attention paid to the preparation of the earth bed. After the foundation is laid the ground is puddled and tamped, puddled and tamped until very firm. Over the surface is spread from four to six inches of sand or sandy loam. Then the concrete is put on. If one part of the floor is below grade, the ground under it is carefully drained, after which the layer of sand prevents moisture from coming through.

The main body of rough concrete should be reinforced to one third of one per cent to prevent cracking, and scored to give a key to the top coat and prevent its loosening from the bottom. The finish coat should be reinforced with number eighteen gauge half-inch mesh galvanized wire to prevent cracking.

From four to six weeks should be allowed for cement floors to dry. During this time there is a continuous process of absorption and radiation of heat until a mean temperature has been reached after which the temperature of the floor is more equable than that of wood.

To cover a cement floor with wood is about as logical as to cover cement sidewalks with boards. Everybody who has lived on cement floors laid according to the given specifications has been wholly converted to them and would never again be bothered with the care and trials of wood floors. It is not, of course, expected that concrete floors should be left bare. They should be partly covered with rugs, the same as a polished wood floor. Incidently, when properly laid, waxed and polished, cement floors are ideal for dancing.

When troweled and finished almost to a gloss, cement floors do not mar or scratch. They should not be scored or marked off into squares or designs. The natural crazing of the top coat is far more pleasing. I have found no cement floor paint that produces a good effect. The hard monotonous flat colors are unpleasing, the paint soon wears off and shows the cement. Instead of using paint I mix color with the cement, usually tones of red and yellow, red and brown or yellow and brown slightly mottled. Tempered by the gray of the cement these colors produce neutral tones that are a splendid background for rugs and furniture. When quite dry, the cement should be cleaned with a weak solution of ammonia and water, given two coats of Chinese nut oil to bring out the color, then finished with a filler and waxed like hardwood. Well done, the treatment gives an effect of old Spanish leather.

It is quite as impossible to tell how to lay and finish a cement floor to bring out all its potential beauty as it is to give exact rules for the painting of a picture. Specifications and instructions carry one just so far, but beyond that point each builder must study out the problem for himself. It takes the knack or the inspiration or the gift—whatever its name—that differentiates craftsmanship from mere mechanical perfection, that raises the artist above the artisan, to make a cement floor the thing of beauty it can and should be.

Before it has set, cement is a wonderfully plastic material, more wonderful than clay. It can be colored, modeled, shaded, surfaced, and then of itself hardens into an everlasting expression of the workman.

The protest against ordinary cement floors is the unconscious demand for the thing well done. At heart we are never satisfied with any work that is not done right, and cement floors will not come into their own until architect and workman study them as an art.

The cement floors in the home of Homer Laughlin in Los Angeles, forecast the possibilities of the future. Sprawling there, his soul in his work, with great sweeps of his trowel an artist wrought in that plastic, responsive material, blending the colors marvelously in the broad central spaces, coaxing them to a rare harmony of tone and exquisite finish, and around the outer edges he carved in low relief the lines of acanthus and other simple conventionalized leaf forms. In the entrance hall, with big free strokes he limned the feather-like fronds of a palm, using his color with consummate skill and an artist's feeling. The appeal of this most modern manifestation of ceramic art is far more subtle than that of the mosaics which were the acme of floor-making among the Greeks and Romans, and it has the singular advantage of being within reach of beauty lovers of moderate means.

Concrete floors are cheaper than wood for the first story, they are enduring, they require a minimum of care, they are comfortable and healthful when laid right, and they can be more beautiful than any other floor.

"The Home of the Future: The New Architecture of the West: Small Homes for a Great Country,"

by Irving J. Gill.

Reprinted from *The Craftsman*, May 1916 (line drawings by Lloyd Wright).

"An artist is known rather by what he omits."

Architecture, Victor Hugo says, is the great book of the world, the principal expression of man in his different stages of development, the chief register of humanity. Every religious symbol, every human thought has its page and its monument in that immense book. Down to the time of Gutenberg, he points out, architecture was the principal, the universal writing. Whoever was born a poet then, became an architect. All arts obeyed and placed themselves under the discipline of architecture. They were the workmen of the great work. There was nothing which, in order to make something of itself, was not forced to frame itself in the shape of architectural hymn or prose. He has shown us that the great products of architecture are less the works of individuals than of society, rather the offspring of a nation's effort than the inspired flash of a man of genius, the deposit left by a whole people, the heaps accumulated by centuries, the residue of successive evaporations of human society, in a word, a species of formation. Each wave of time contributes its alluvium, each race deposits its layer on the monument, each individual brings his stone.

No architect can read his inspired analysis of the place and the importance of architecture in preserving the records of the world's thought and action, without approaching his own part in this human record with a greater reverence and greater sense of responsibility. What rough or quarried stone will each of us contribute to the universal edifice, what idle or significant sentence will we write with brick and stone, wood, steel and concrete upon the sensitive page of the earth? In California we have great wide plains, arched by blue skies that are fresh chapters as yet unwritten. We have noble mountains, lovely little hills and canyons waiting to hold the record of this generation's history, ideals, imagination, sense of romance and honesty. What monument will we who build, erect to the honor or shame of our age?

The West has an opportunity unparalleled in the history of the world, for it is the newest white page turned for registration. The present builders have the advantage of all the wisdom and experience of the ages to aid them in poetically inscribing today's milestone in the progress of humanity. The West unfortunately has been and is building too hastily, carelessly and thoughtlessly. Houses are springing up faster than mushrooms, for mushrooms silently prepare for a year and more before they finally raise their house above the ground in proof of what they have been designing so long and secretly. People pour out here as on the crest of a flood and remain where chance deposits them when the rush of waters subsides, building temporary shacks wherein they live for a brief period while looking about for more permanent anchorage. The surface of the ground is barely scraped away, in some cases but a few inches deep, just enough to allow builders to find a level, and a house is tossed together with little thought of beauty, and no thought of permanence, haste being the chief characteristic. The family of health-or fortune-seekers who comes out here generally expects to camp in these poor shacks for but a short time and plans to sell the shiftless affair to some other impatient newcomer. Perhaps such temporary proceedings are necessary in the settling of a new land; fortunately such structures cannot endure, will never last long enough to be a monument for future generations to wonder at. Such structures cannot rightly be called homes, so do not justly deserve notice in consideration as Western domestic architecture.

If we, the architects of the West, wish to do great and lasting work we must dare to be simple, must have the courage to fling aside every device that distracts the eye from structural beauty, must break through convention and get down to fundamental truths. Through force of custom and education we, in whose hands much of the beauty of country and city is entrusted, have been compelled to study the style of other men, with the result that most of our modern work is an open imitation or veiled plagiarism of another's idea. To break away from this degradation we must boldly throw aside every accepted structural belief and standard of beauty and get back to the source of all architectural strength—the straight line, the arch, the cube and the circle—and drink from these fountains of Art that gave life to the great men of old.

Every artist must sooner or later reckon directly, personally with these four principles—the mightiest of lines. The straight line borrowed from the horizon is a symbol of greatness, grandeur and nobility; the arch patterned from the dome of the sky represents exultation, reverence, aspiration; the circle is the sign of completeness, motion and progression, as may be seen when a stone touches water; the square is the symbol of power, justice, honesty and firmness. These are the bases, the units of architectural language, and without them there can be no direct or inspired architectural speech. We must not weaken our message of beauty and strength by the stutter and mumble of useless ornaments. If we have nothing worth while to say with our building then we should keep quiet. Why should we chatter idly and meaninglessly with foolish ornaments and useless lines?

Any deviation from simplicity results in a loss of dignity. Ornaments tend to cheapen rather than enrich, they acknowledge inefficiency and weakness. A house cluttered up by complex ornament means that the designer was aware that his work lacked purity of line and perfection of proportion, so he endeavored to cover its imperfection by adding on detail, hoping thus to distract the attention of the observer from the fundamental weakness of his design. If we omit everything useless from the structural point of view we will come to see the great beauty of straight lines, to see the charm that lies in perspective, the force in light and shade, the power in balanced masses, the fascination of color that plays upon a smooth wall left free to report the passing of a cloud or nearness of a flower, the furious rush of storms and the burning stillness of summer suns. We would also see the glaring defects of our own work if left in this bold, unornamented fashion, and therefore could swiftly correct it.

I believe if we continually think more of line, proportion, light and shade, we will reach greater skill in handling them, and a greater appreciation and understanding of their power and beauty. We should build our house simple, plain and substantial as a boulder, then leave the ornamentation of it to Nature, who will tone it with lichens, chisel it with storms, make it gracious and friendly with vines and flower shadows as she does the stone in the meadow. I believe also that houses should be built more substantially and should be made absolutely sanitary. If the cost of unimportant ornamentation were put into construction, then we would have a more lasting and a more dignified architecture.

In California we have long been experimenting with the idea of producing a perfectly sanitary, labor-saving house, one where the maximum of comfort may be had with the minimum of drudgery. In the recent houses that I have built the walls are finished flush with the casings and the line where the wall joins the flooring is slightly rounded, so that it forms one continuous piece with no place for dust to enter or to lodge, or crack for vermin of any kind to exist. There is no molding for pictures, plates or chairs, no baseboards, paneling or wainscoting to catch and hold the dust. The doors are single slabs of hand polished mahogany swung on invisible hinges or else made so that they slide in the wall. In some of the houses all windows and door frames are of steel. They never wear out, warp or burn, a point of importance in fireproof construction. The drain boards are sunk in magnesite which is made in one piece with the walls and all cornices rounded, so not a particle of grease or dirt can lodge, or

dampness collect and become unwholesome. The bathtubs are boxed and covered with magnesite up to the porcelain.

By this manner of building there is no chance anywhere in the house for dust to accumulate. This minimizes the labor of keeping the house clean and gives the rooms a sweet, pure, simple and dignified appearance. The money usually wasted in meaningless gables, swags, machine-made garlands, fretwork and "gingerbread" goes into labor-saving devices or into better grade of material. As much thought goes into the placing of the ice-box that can be filled from the outside without tracking through a clean kitchen, or the letter box that can be opened from within the house, or the proper disposal of the garbage can, or the convenient arrangement of kitchens so that meals may be prepared with the greatest economy of labor, as is often expended in the planning of the pergola or drawing rooms.

There is something very restful and satisfying to my mind in the simple cube house with creamy walls, sheer and plain, rising boldly into the sky, unrelieved by cornices or overhang of roof, unornamented save for the vines that soften a line or creepers that wreathe a pillar or flowers that inlay color more sentiently than any tile could do. I like the bare honesty of these houses, the childlike frankness and chaste simplicity of them. It seemed too peculiar an innovation at first to make a house without a large overhang roof, for we have been so accustomed in California to think them a necessity, but now that the first shock is over people welcome the simplicity of the houses built without these heavy overhangs and see that they really have distinction.

In the West, home building has followed, in the main, two distinct lines—the Spanish Mission and the India bungalow. True, we find many small Swiss châlets clinging perilously to canyon walls, imposing Italian villas facing the sea and myriad nameless creations whose chief distinction lies in the obvious fact that they are original, different from any known type of architecture. It were much

better for California if there were less complicated, meaningless originality and more frank following of established good types.

Because of the intense blue of sky and sea that continues for such long, unbroken periods, the amethyst distant mountains that form an almost universal background for houses or cities, the golden brown of summer fields, the varied green of pepper, eucalyptus and poplar trees that cut across it in such decorative forms and the profusion of gay flowers that grow so quickly and easily, houses of a bright romantic picturesqueness are perfectly suitable that would seem too dramatic in other parts of the country. They seem a pleasing part of the orange-belted flower fields and belong to the semi-tropical land. These same houses would certainly look artificial and amusingly uncomfortable and out of place in the East; but they essentially belong to the land of sunshine.

The contour, coloring and history of a country naturally influence its architecture. The old wooden Colonial houses of the East, shaded by noble elms, with their attendant lanes and roads outlined by stone walls, perfect pictures of home beauty; the stone houses of Pennsylvania, charming of color, stately, eloquent of substantial affluence and generous hospitality; and the adobe houses of the Arizona Indians formed of the earth into structures so like the surrounding ledges and buttes in shape that they can scarcely be told from them, triumphs of protective, harmonious building, are familiar types of buildings characteristic of their locality.

California is influenced, and rightly so, by the Spanish Missions as well as by the rich coloring and the form of the low hills and wide valleys. The Missions are a part of its history that should be preserved and in their long, low lines, graceful arcades, tile roofs, bell towers, arched doorways and walled gardens we find a most expressive medium of retaining tradition, history and romance. In coloring and general form they are exactly suited to the romantic requirements of the country. It is safe to say that more architectural crimes have been committed in their name than in any other unless it be the Grecian temples. The façade of the San Diego Mission is a wonderful thing, something that deserves to be a revered model, something to which local building might safely and advantageously have been keyed. Instead of this it has been abused and caricatured in the most shocking way. Its charming proportions and graceful outline have been distorted to adorn tall public buildings, low railway stations, ornate hotels, cramped stables and minute private houses in the most irreverent, inexcusable and pitiable way. The arched cloisters of the Missions have been seized upon and tortured until all semblance of their original beauty has been lost. Their meaning and definite purpose—that of supporting the roof or the second story and thus forming a retreat or quiet walk for the monks—has been almost forgotten.

The arch is one of our most imposing, most picturesque and graceful architectural features. Its power of creating beauty is unquestionable, but like any other great force, wrongly used, is equally destructive. Fire warms and cheers us and cooks our food, but if not carefully handled destroys everything it touches. The Missions have taught us also the beauty and usefulness of the court. Romana's house [sic, "Ramona's house," actually Casa de Estudillo], a landmark as familiar in the South as some of the Missions, was built around three sides of an open space, the other side being a high garden wall. This home plan gave privacy, protection and beauty. The court contains a pool and well in the center and an arbor for grapes along the garden wall; the archway that runs along the three sides formed by the house made the open-air living rooms. Here were arranged couches for sleeping, hammocks for the siesta, easy chairs and tables for dining. There was always a sheltered and a sunny side, always seclusion and an outlook into the garden. In California we have liberally borrowed this home plan, for it is hard to devise a better, cozier, more convenient or practical scheme for a home. In the seclusion of the outdoor living rooms and in their nearness to the garden, the arrangement is ideal.

Another thing that has influenced California architecture is the redwood that is so abundant and so different from anything in the East. In color it is a low-toned red that looks as though it were lighted by sun rays. It blends harmoniously with the clear atmosphere of the country, it is inexpensive, easily handled and outlasts almost any known wood, for it does not rot when standing in the ground nor when subject to continued dampness. Split into long, narrow shingles called shakes, or into long clapboards, it makes strikingly beautiful houses. Furniture of simple lines is also made of it, and though it is frequently oiled or varnished or bitten by acids to a soft gray tone it is more often left in its own lusterless beauty. Redwood houses look as natural a part of the forest and canyon as a tawny mushroom or gray stone. Delightful little home-made cottages of redwood are to be found all through California. They cost their owners but a few hundred dollars. These camps or week-end houses are the very apple of the people's eye. Everybody has one and lives therein happier than any king, enjoying a simple, free, healthy life, breathing eucalyptus and pine-scented air, resting full length in flower-starred grass, bathing in the fern-bordered streams. As contrast to these myriads of comfortable, lovable little camp homes that can be built for three or four hundred dollars, and that look as picturesque and fascinating as any bird's nest, are beautiful palaces of concrete for people possessed of many acres, built with every modern convenience and every device for creating beauty, with fountains, swimming pools, sun parlors, outdoor dancing courts and lawn, pergolas, tea houses, art galleries and a thousand other wonderful things that contribute to elaborate and luxurious living.

List of Known Projects

An asterisk (*) indicates that the date or architectural firm has not yet been verified by documentary evidence. All buildings are in California unless otherwise noted, and their present status is given when known. Below the name is a code for the architectural firm, according to the following list. The arrangement may not have been a formal partnership in each case.

B & G	Horatio Warren Bishop and Irving Gill	G & M	Irving Gill and Frank Mead
F & G	Joseph Falkenham and Irving Gill	G & P	Irving Gill and Pearson
G	Irving Gill	I & G	Alfonso Iannelli and Irving Gill
G & A	Irving Gill and Frank Allen	H & G	William Hebbard and Irving Gill
G G & A	Bertram Goodhue, Irving Gill, and Frank Allen	H G & K	William Hebbard, Irving Gill, and Edward Kent
G & G	Irving Gill and Louis Gill	S & G	John Siebert and Irving Gill

1893

Daniel Schuyler residence
G—SW corner 25th and E, San Diego (restored)

Hotel
G—Golden Hill, San Diego (not built)

John Kendall residence (Waverly Ranch)
G—Hillside, El Cajon

1894

Gerichten-Choate-Peterson Building
F & G—832 5th, San Diego (restored)

Dunston Block
F & G—NE corner 7th and E, San Diego

Mrs. M. A. Wilcox residence
F & G—NW corner 2nd and B, San Diego (gone)

Mr. Parson Shaw residence
F & G—Quince and Fourth, San Diego

S. W. Belding residence (alterations)
F & G—D (Broadway) and 18th, San Diego (gone)

French Laundry
F & G—Plaza, San Diego

Major Miles Moylan residence
F & G—2220 2nd, San Diego (restored)

Edward M. Burbeck cottage (#1)
F & G—Prospect, La Jolla

Graham & Steiner Building
F & G—Grand and Lime, Escondido (demolished)

Gustave W. Jorres residence
F & G—San Diego

M. Garman residence (alterations)
F & G—3rd and Fir, San Diego

Eugene W. Britt residence (interior alterations)
F & G—NE corner Fourth and Maple, San Diego (intact)

Four Cabrillo Arches
F & G—Escondido (temporary structure for parade)

A. B. Standers residence
F & G—3rd and A, San Diego

W. J. Prout residence
F & G—Wynola Ranch, Julian

Dr. Hearne office
F & G—4th and Ash, San Diego (gone)

Fair building
F & G—Fairgrounds, San Diego

N. McKee residence
F & G—La Jolla

John Kendall cottage ("Windemere")
F & G—1328 Virginia Way, La Jolla (intact)

"The Green Dragon" for Anna Held*
G*—Prospect, La Jolla (demolished)

1895

Tallie Spencer residence
F & G—lot 27, block 136, Chula Vista

J. R. Harning residence
G—San Diego

H. W. Nichols residence
G—Coronado

Mr. Gail Nichols residence*
G—750 Adella, Coronado (burned 1981)

David K. Horton residence
G—1504 22nd, National City (intact)

Rev. Solomon Milne residence
G—844 Juniper (at Front), San Diego (gone)

1896

Goodman residence
G—Coronado

G. George Garrettson residence
G—2410 E (at 24th), San Diego (nearly intact)

Abel H. Frost residence
G—2456 Broadway, San Diego (restored)

Granger Music Hall
G—moved to 4th, east of Palm, National City (restored)

George M. Hawley residence
G—206 Kalmia (at 2nd), San Diego (gone)

Mary Cossitt residence (#1)*
G*—cut in two and moved to 1710 and 1718 Visalia Row, Coronado (remodeled)

Edward M. Burbeck residence
H & G—2352 1st (near Kalmia), San Diego (gone)

Gray residence
H & G—1st near Cedar, San Diego (gone)

Dr. Cotton residence
H & G—University Heights, San Diego

1897

Thomas N. Boutelle residence
H & G—1470 7th (at Beech), San Diego (gone)

Richelieu Building (alterations)
H & G—5th between C and D, San Diego

Los Baños Bathhouse
H & G—735 West D (Broadway), San Diego (demolished 1927)

T. P. Griffith residence
H & G—San Diego

San Diego Land & Town Company Building
H & G—National City

John Osborn residence*
H & G*—2073 Logan, San Diego (intact)

McKenzie, Flint & Winsby Corporation
H & G—SE corner 5th and K, San Diego (intact)

H. H. Bancroft Block
H & G—5th and A, San Diego

Alfred E. Nutt residence
H & G—4th and Walnut, San Diego (gone)

1897-98

John H. Kleine residence (#1, "La Colina")
H & G—9627 Prospect, Lakeside (remodeled)

1898-04

State Normal School
H & G—Campus and Normal, San Diego (demolished 1955)

1898

U. S. Grant, Jr., commercial building
H & G—4th north of D (Broadway), San Diego (demolished)

Anson P. Stephens residence
H & G—711 A, Coronado (greatly enlarged)

Mendell C. Churchill residence
H & G—moved to SE corner 4th and Orange, Coronado (remodeled)

Kindergarten
H & G—Sherman Heights, San Diego (demolished)

Mrs. Margaret Carroll residence
H & G—3770 5th, San Diego (gone)

Ernest E. White
H & G—136 Redwood (at 2nd), San Diego (restored)

Mrs. H. L. Shepard residence (alterations)
H & G—Lot K, Block 212, San Diego

Mary C. Pratt residence*
H & G*—1517 Inez Place, Coronado (remodeled)

Mary Cossitt cottage (#2)
H & G—1037 Star Park Circle, Coronado
(remodeled)

1899

Mary Cossitt cottage (#3)
H & G—1127 Flora, Coronado (entrance remodeled)

Mrs. P. O. Josse commercial building
H & G*—SE corner 5th and D (Broadway), San
Diego (demolished)

First Congregational Church
H & G—Olive Ave., Redlands (intact)

Mrs. E. S. Babcock residence
H & G—Coronado

George Kroenert residence*
H & G*—1471 8th, San Diego (intact)

Mission San Diego de Alcalá (stabilization)
H & G—Mission Valley, San Diego (restored in 1930)

San Diego Cuyamaca & Eastern Depot*
H & G—corner 22nd and M (Imperial), San Diego
(gone)

1900

Wednesday Club
H & G—6th and Thornton (Pennsylvania), San Diego
(gone)

Bowen Block for Southwest Investment Co.
H & G—5th between C and D (Broadway), San Diego
(remodeled)

Public Library (supervisors for Ackerman & Ross,
NY)
H & G—E between 8th and 9th, San Diego
(demolished)

Mills residence*
H & G*—1604 7th (at Cedar), San Diego (intact)

Waldo Waterman residence ("Granite Cottage")
H & G—237 W. Hawthorne, San Diego (nearly
intact)

Irving Gill cottage
H & G—Robinson and University (?), San Diego

1900-01

Elwyn B. Gould residence
H & G—234 W. Juniper, San Diego (demolished
1987)

Albert H. Olmsted residence ("Wildacre")
H & G—Ocean Ave., Newport, RI (nearly intact)

1901

J. C. Hizer residence
H & G—1135 Loma, Coronado (gone)

George McKenzie residence
H & G—208 W. Kalmia (at Front), San Diego
(demolished)

Joseph Sefton commercial building
H & G—4th and C, San Diego

Miss Mary A. Sterrett residence
H & G—542 22nd, San Diego (intact)

San Diego Gas Works (alterations)
H & G—San Diego

Miss Emma Frances Way residence
H & G—419 Redwood (at 4th), San Diego (gone)

La Jolla Tavern
H & G—La Jolla (not built)

1901-02

Bartlett Richards residence
H & G—1015 Ocean Blvd., Coronado (greatly
enlarged)

1902

All Saints Church and Rectory
H & G—6th and Thornton (Pennsylvania), San Diego
(built?)

Zlac Rowing Club
H & G—foot of H, San Diego (built?)

Road Houses (log cabins) for San Diego Flume
Company
H & G—San Diego County (built?)

San Diego Cuyamaca and Eastern Railroad Company
H & G—foot of 10th, San Diego (alterations)

Miss Sarah Birkhead residence*
H & G—Portsmouth, RI

Miss Ellen Mason residence
H & G—Newport, RI (now St. Michael's School)

Fifth Ward School
H & G—NE corner Union and F, San Diego
(demolished)

North Chollas School
H & G—San Diego (built?)

Music Stand
H & G—Golden Hill (Balboa) Park, San Diego
(built?)

Louis Fritz residence
H & G—1572 1st, San Diego (gone)

Johnson Puterbaugh residence
H & G—2970 2nd (at Quince), San Diego (intact)

Irving Gill cottage
H & G—4th near Robinson, San Diego

El Cajon Presbyterian Church
H & G—El Cajon (demolished)

1903

Mrs. Shaw-Safe residence*
H & G—East Greenwich, RI

Louis B. McCagg residence ("Woodlands")
H & G—Bar Harbor, ME (burned 1947)

George Tammen residence
H & G—2419 H (Market), San Diego (gone?)

Mrs. Ida D. Chappell residence
H & G—231 Ivy, San Diego (gone)

Capt. W. Mifflin Smith residence (alterations)
H & G—2508 1st (at Laurel), San Diego (restored)

Irving Gill cottage
H & G—3709 Albatross, San Diego (remodeled)

Irving Gill cottage*
H & G*—3703 Albatross, San Diego (Gill listed at this
address in 1905, but house now at this address looks
later than 1905)

San Diego Yacht Club
H & G—San Diego (built?)

Hotel Robinson (alterations, former Florence Hotel)
H & G—Fir from 3rd to 4th, San Diego (demolished)

Mrs. Marion L. Wincote residence
H & G—3720 7th, San Diego (intact)

Herbert E. Anthony residence
H & G—3554 2nd, San Diego (gone)

Unidentified business block
H & G—6th and H (Market), San Diego (built?)

J. O. Smith residence
H & G—Palo Alto, CA (not built)

Mrs. Henry residence
H & G—Hollywood, CA (not built)

Mrs. George Noble Todd residence
H & G—Hemet, CA (not built)

William O. Bowen residence
H & G—3rd and Walnut, San Diego (built?)

Edward C. Burbeck cottage (#2)
H & G—La Jolla, CA

John Gay commercial building
H & G—6th near D (Broadway), San Diego

Capt. Clarke cottage
H & G—La Jolla, CA (built?)

Edward Mayer residence
H & G—5th and Juniper, San Diego

Post Office (alterations)
H & G—San Diego

William H. Porterfield residence
H & G—SW corner 2nd and Upas, San Diego (not
built, date on drawings is unclear, could be 1905)

1904

Children's Home (addition)
H & G—upper 15th, San Diego (demolished)

Frederick H. Moses flower shop
H & G—123 Main, Bar Harbor, ME (nearly intact)

William Stewart residence
H & G—942 23rd, San Diego (remodeled)

Walter B. Woodward apartments
H & G—7th between D (Broadway) and C, San Diego
(gone)

E. Milton Barber residence (#1)
H & G—108 W. Robinson (at 1st), San Diego
(remodeled)

American National Bank (alterations for Louis Wilde)
H & G—5th near C, San Diego

Warren M. Crouse residence
H & G—San Diego (built?)

Judge Monroe B. Anderson residence
H & G—Front near Juniper, San Diego (built?)

Mrs. Prentice apartments
H & G—4th between Date and Elm, San Diego
(built?)

1904-05

George W. Marston residence
H & G—3525 7th, San Diego (intact, public museum)

Bertha B. Mitchell residence
H & G—2720 4th (at Nutmeg), San Diego
(remodeled)

First Church of Christ Scientist (#1)
H & G—SE corner 3rd and Ash, San Diego (nearly
intact)

Pickwick Theatre (for Louis Wilde)
H & G—1029 4th, San Diego (gone)

Irving Gill cottage
H & G—2488 L (near 25th), San Diego (remodeled)

Irving Gill cottage
H & G—SW corner 25th and L, San Diego
(remodeled)

1904-06

Julius Wangenheim residence
H & G—148 W. Juniper, San Diego (demolished
1965)

1905

Public Fountain
H & G—Girard near Prospect, La Jolla (gone)

Fifth Ward School (alterations)
H & G—NE corner Union and F, San Diego
(demolished)

John Olmsted residence*
H & G—Chepiwanoxet (East Greenwich), RI

unidentified residence*
H & G—Apponaug (East Greenwich), RI

Taber Block
H & G—4th north of D (Broadway), San Diego
(built?)

U. S. Grant, Jr., Block
H & G—4th north of D (Broadway), San Diego

Escondido National Bank (for Louis Wilde)
H & G—Escondido

Hotel for Guajome Health Company
H & G—Rancho Guajome, San Luis Rey (not built)

Clubhouse and conservatory for Ellen Scripps
H & G—700 Prospect, La Jolla (gone)

Gateway for South Moulton Villa (for Ellen Scripps)
H & G—700 Prospect, La Jolla (gone)

Biological Station, La Jolla
H & G—cut in two and moved, one part behind 7467
Girard

William S. Hebbard residence
H & G—2800 3rd (at Olive), San Diego (demolished)

Samuel L. Wood residence
H & G—2412 C, San Diego (substantially remodeled)

S. H. Embrey residence
H & G—corner 6th and Maple, San Diego (built?)

Charles S. Hamilton residence
H & G—3575 6th, San Diego (remodeled into
apartments)

Charles P. Douglas res. (AKA Mary Johnson res.)
H & G—202 Nutmeg (at 2nd), San Diego
(demolished)

La Jolla School
H & G—La Jolla (gone)

Hotel to replace Horton House
H G & K–D (Broadway) between 3rd and 4th, San
Diego (not built)

1905-06

Alice Lee residence (#1, McCoy #3)
H & G—3574 7th, San Diego (nearly intact)

Alice Lee cottage (#2, McCoy #1)
H & G—3578 7th, San Diego (intact)

Katherine Teats (#1)
H & G—3560 7th, San Diego (remodeled by Louis
Gill)

La Jolla Bathhouse
H & G—La Jolla (demolished)

YMCA Gymnasium
H & G—San Diego (demolished)

1905-07

San Diego First Methodist Church
H & G—NW corner 9th and C, San Diego
(demolished 1965)

1906

Irving Gill cottage*
H & G—3776 Front, San Diego (nearly intact)

Mary Cossitt residence(#4)
H & G—3526 7th, San Diego (nearly intact)

Frederick R. Burnham residence
H & G—3565 7th, San Diego (somewhat remodeled)

Frank W. Barnes residence
H & G—3405 4th, San Diego (gone)

Gustav Breslin
H & G—2078 University, San Diego (gone)

Mrs. Ermina Carrington residence
H & G—3344 5th, San Diego (gone)

Mrs. S. Forman residence
H & G—Coronado (built?)

University Heights School
H & G—San Diego (competition awarded to H. L.
Gay)

Sam Ferry Smith residence
H & G—2222 4th, San Diego (totally remodeled)

Edmund F. Parmelee residence
H & G—202 W. Ivy (at Front), San Diego (totally
remodeled)

Dr. Homer C. Oatman residence
H & G—2437 2nd, San Diego (remodeled)

Mrs. Margaret Tripp residence (alterations)
H & G—3024 5th, San Diego (gone)

Mrs. J. Wade MacDonald residence
H & G—5th north of Upas, San Diego (gone)

George W. Craine residence
H & G—Redwood at Park (6th), San Diego (not
built)

Bernard W. McKenzie residence
H & G*—7th & Thornton (Pennsylvania), San Diego
(built?)

San Diego Woman's Club
H & G—949 9th, south of D (Broadway), San Diego
(gone)

Apartment building for Miss Peckham
H & G—San Diego (built?)

Apartment building for Edwin A. Wells
H & G—San Diego (built?)

John H. Kleine residence (#2)*
H & G*—moved to Channel Rd. at Julian, Lakeside
(restored)

1906-07

Louis J. Wilde residence
H & G—5th near Juniper, San Diego (not built)

Germania Hall
H & G—SW corner 9th and G, San Diego
(demolished)

Hotel Crane
H & G—1127 5th between B and C, San Diego
(demolished)

1907

George M. Hawley residence
H & G—4744 Panorama Dr., San Diego (intact)

Lanier Hotel (completed by Hebbard)
H & G—NE corner 3rd and Ash, San Diego
(demolished)

Dr. H. Nevill Goff residence
H & G—3580 5th, San Diego (demolished)

I. Isaac Irwin residence (completed by Gill)
H & G—535 Date (at 6th), San Diego (demolished)

unidentified apartment building (competition)
H & G—7th to 8th, A to B, San Diego (not built)

Wheeler J. Bailey residence ("Hilerô")
G & M—7964 Princess, La Jolla (enlarged by Gill)

William E. Smythe residence
G & M—Hillcrest Dr., San Diego (not built)

Russell C. Allen residence
G & M—4094 Old Orchard Ln., Bonita (intact)

Children's Home Association (alterations)
G & M—upper 15th, San Diego (demolished)

Virginia Scripps (alterations)
G—La Jolla

1907-08

Melville Klauber residence
G & M—3060 6th (at Redwood), San Diego
(demolished 1979)

Homer Laughlin, Jr., residence
G—666 W. 28th, Los Angeles (demolished)

St. James Chapel
G—moved to Draper and Genter, La Jolla (nearly
intact)

1908

Omega Port Memorial Fountain
G—Mt. Hope Cemetery, San Diego (demolished
1991)

Irving Gill cottage*
G—3719 Albatross, San Diego (remodeled into
3721?)

Irving Gill cottages*
G*—2119 & 2123 Albatross, San Diego (intact)

Irving Gill cottage*
G*—220 W. Hawthorne, San Diego (remodeled)

Irving Gill cottage*
G—3733 Robinson Mews, San Diego (intact)

Irving Gill cottage
G—3755 Robinson Mews, San Diego (intact with
addition)

Sherwood Wheaton residence
G—3102 6th (at Redwood), San Diego (demolished
1979)

Newell H. Webster residence
G—1516 7th (at Beech), San Diego (demolished)

Wilson-Acton Hotel (AKA Hotel Cabrillo)
G—1116 Prospect, La Jolla (remodeled, now part of
La Valencia Hotel)

Propagating house for Ellen Scripps
G—700 Prospect, La Jolla (demolished)

Guest cottage for Ellen Scripps
G—moved to 2491 Horizon, La Jolla (intact)

J. H. Williams summerhouse (log cabin)
G—California Springs, Tulare County (built?)

Hugo Klauber residence
G—2626 6th, San Diego (totally remodeled)

Thomas Hamilton residence (AKA Mary Fulford res.)
G—3500 7th, San Diego (demolished)

1908-09

John P. Christensen Flats
G—312 22nd, San Diego (nearly intact)

Peter M. Price residence (#1)
G—1355 Granada (at Ash), San Diego (nearly intact)

Peter M. Price cottage(#2)
G—1345 Granada, San Diego (intact)

Peter M. Price cottage (#3)
G—1331 Granada, San Diego (intact)

Annie B. Darst Flats (#1)
G—2266 5th (at Juniper), San Diego (intact)

Annie B. Darst residence
G—NE corner 5th and Kalmia, San Diego
(demolished)

Boys' Dormitory, Children's Home Association
G—upper 15th, San Diego (demolished)

1908-10

Scripps Biological Station
G—Scripps Inst. of Oceanography, La Jolla (restored)

1909

Annie B. Darst Flats (#2)
G—5th north of Kalmia, San Diego (demolished)

Holly Sefton Memorial Hospital, Children's Home Association
G—upper 15th, San Diego (demolished)

Bank Building
G—La Mesa (built?)

The Bishop's Day School
G—3012 1st, San Diego (intact)

Albert B. Curtis residence
G—Playa del Sur, La Jolla

George Clark residence
G—La Jolla Strand, La Jolla

Pavilion and Clubhouse
G—La Jolla Strand, La Jolla (built?)

E. Milton Barber residence(#2)
G—3934 3rd, San Diego (remodeled)

G. W. Simmons residence
G—3506 Albatross, San Diego (remodeled)

Arthur H. Marston residence
G—3575 7th, San Diego (enlarged by Louis Gill)

YMCA
G—8th and C, San Diego (not built)

Plan for Plaza (later named Horton Plaza)
G—D (Broadway), 3rd to 4th, San Diego (restored)

1909-10

First Church of Christ Scientist (#2)
G—corner 2nd and Laurel, San Diego (to be restored)

Mrs. Harriet P. Thurston residence
G—Silvergate (Pt. Loma), San Diego (not built)

1910

Electric Fountain for the Plaza
G—D (Broadway), 3rd to 4th, San Diego (restored)

Scripps Hall, The Bishop's School
G—7607 La Jolla Blvd., La Jolla (nearly intact)

Bentham Hall, The Bishop's School
G—7607 La Jolla Blvd., La Jolla (nearly intact)

Fannie M. McKoon residence
G—2204 Albatross (at Ivy), San Diego (remodeled)

F. B. Lewis Court ("Bella Vista Terrace")
G—Mt. Trail and Alegria, Sierra Madre (remodeled)

Dr. Charles L. Tutt residence
G—1007 Ocean Blvd., Coronado (remodeled)

Mary Cossitt cottages (#5, #6, #7 & #8)
G—3729, 3735, 3749, 3757 8th, San Diego (#7 remodeled)

George Steckel residence
G—Los Angeles (plans marked "void")

San Diego Country Club
G—1740 Upas, San Diego (demolished)

1910-11

Percival Thompson residence
G—1156 Isabella, Coronado (house intact, rear yard lost)

C. L. Gorham residence
G—SW corner 6th and Olive, San Diego (demolished)

Alterations to National City High School
G—10th and F, National City (demolished)

Sefton cottage and pottery plant (Valentien Pottery)
G—3911 Texas (at University), San Diego (demolished)

1911

Henry H. Timken residence
G—335 Walnut (at 4th), San Diego (demolished)

Additions to Alice Lee cottage (#2)
G—3578 7th, San Diego (intact)

Gate for Rafaelle Lorini (former Mary Pratt res.)
G—1517 Inez Pl, Coronado

Paul Miltimore residence
G—1301 S. Chelton Way, South Pasadena (intact)

Marion Olmsted residence
G—Hooker and Stockton, San Diego (plans marked "void")

1911-12

Nelson E. Barker residence
G—306 Walnut, San Diego (demolished)

Bethel African Methodist Episcopal Church
G—1649 Front, San Diego (gone)

Administration Building, Panama-California Exposition
G G & A—Balboa Park, San Diego (restored)

1912

Las Flores Hotel (for Roscoe Hazard)
G—4th between F and G, San Diego (remodeled)

Echo Park Court*
G*—Los Angeles (demolished)

Mrs. George D. Ruddy residence
G—Los Angeles

Katherine Teats cottage (#2)
G—3415 Albatross, San Diego (nearly intact)

Alice Lee cottage (#3, McCoy #4)
G—3367 Albatross, San Diego (intact)

Katherine Teats cottage (#3)
G—3407 Albatross, San Diego (intact)

Store and Hotel Building (to replace St. James Hotel)
G & A—F between 6th and 7th, San Diego (not built)

Casas Grandes apartments* (for Homer Laughlin)
G—Franklin, Center and Felis, Los Angeles (not built)

Frank C. O'Kelly residence
G—SE corner 1st and Olive, San Diego (not built)

1912-13

Ellen B. Scripps library
G—700 Prospect, La Jolla (gone)

Frank J. Belcher, Jr., residence
G—241 W. Kalmia (at Albatross), San Diego (demolished)

Office Building
G—El Prado at Cabrillo, Torrance (demolished)

Commercial Building
G—1610 Cabrillo, Torrance

School
G—Torrance (demolished)

Murray Hotel
G—1210 El Prado, Torrance

Rubbercraft Corporation of California
G—1800 W. 220th, Torrance

Workers' housing
G—1815, 1819, 1903, 1904, 1907, 1916, 1919, 1920 Gramercy, Torrance

Fuller Shoe Manufacturing Company
G—1860 Torrance Blvd, Torrance

Torrance Bridge
G—near Torrance & Western, Torrance

Brighton Hotel
G—1639 Cabrillo, Torrance

United Cigar Store, Colonial Hotel
G—1601-05 Cabrillo, Torrance

Pacific Electric Depot
G—1200 Cabrillo, Torrance

Salm Manufacturing Company
G—1805 Abalone, Torrance

El Roi Tan Hotel
G—1210 El Prado, Torrance

1912-14

La Jolla Woman's Club
G—715 Silverado, La Jolla (altered by Louis Gill)

1913

Alice Lee cottage(#4, McCoy #2)
G—3353 Albatross, San Diego (nearly intact)

E. G. Sherman Flats (eight apartments)
G—Park at Lemoyne, Los Angeles

Mrs. M. N. Brochon residence
G—Lake near Mountain, Los Angeles

Workers' barracks, Riverside Portland Cement Company
G—Crestmore (gone)

Mrs. Sarah R. Clark residence
G—7731 Hillside, Hollywood

W. C. Powers Flats (four apartments)
G—823-827 S. New Hampshire, Los Angeles

George Kautz residence
G—7753 Draper, La Jolla (restored with large addition)

1913-14

Mrs. Mary H. Banning residence
G—513 S. Commonwealth, Los Angeles (demolished)

Structures for Banning Farmstead*
G—Wilmington

Banning buildings*
G—Catalina Island

Tower Project*
I & G—Pacific Beach, San Diego (not built)

1914

Miss Adelaide M. Chapin residence
G—Lucille near Reservoir, Los Angeles

1914-15

Scripps Playground director's cottage
G & G—Cuvier St, La Jolla (gone)

Homer Laughlin Theatre
G—4th and Pine, Long Beach (demolished)

Exhibition booth, Panama-Pacific International Exposition
G—San Francisco (temporary structure for fair)

1914-16

Walter L. Dodge residence
G—950 Kings Rd., West Hollywood (demolished 1970)

Scripps Playground and Recreation Center
G & G—615 Prospect, La Jolla (nearly intact)

1915

Casas Grandes apartments for Homer Laughlin*
G—Los Angeles (not built)

1915-16

Ellen B. Scripps residence
G—700 Prospect, La Jolla (totally remodeled)

1916

Margerum residence*
G & G—Elizabethville, PA (not built)

St. James Rectory
G & G—La Jolla (not built)

Hospital
G & G—upper 5th, San Diego (not built)

1916-17

Gilman Hall, The Bishop's School
G & G—7607 La Jolla Blvd., La Jolla (intact)

1917

Morgan residence*
G—626 N. Arden (at Melrose), Hollywood (restored)

1917-18

West Adams Villa apartments
G—Pasadena

1918

unidentified residence* (AKA Samuel Raymond res.)
G*—2749 E. Ocean, Long Beach

1919

Horatio West Court*
G—126 Hollister, Santa Monica (largely restored)

Louis Wilde Flats (two apartments)
G & G—corner D and Palm, Coronado (intact, roofline altered)

1919-20

Church of the Sacred Heart
G & G—corner 7th and C, Coronado (intact, dome tiled)

1919-21

Kate Crane Gartz duplex
G—950 N. Oakland, Pasadena (restored)

1920-22

Chauncey Dwight Clarke residence
G—10211 Pioneer Blvd., Santa Fe Springs (intact)

1921

J. D. L. Chandler apartments
G & P—1105-07 4th, Santa Monica

1922-23

J. Harvey McCarthy residence (#1)
B & G—Del Valle Dr. (near Fairfax), Los Angeles

J. Harvey McCarthy residence (#2)
B & G—6336 Warner Dr., Los Angeles

William S. Lord residence (#2)
B & G—Warner Dr. (near Fairfax), Los Angeles

William C. Humburch residence (#1)
B & G—lot 477, Schumacher Dr., Los Angeles

William C. Humburch residence (#2)
B & G—lots 159 & 160, Del Valle Dr., Los Angeles

C. R. Bell residence
B & G—Warner Dr. (near McCarthy Vista), Los Angeles

1924

Arthur J. Misner residence
G—6611 Woodward, Bell (remodeled)

1925

unidentified apartment building
G—no location (not built)

1927-28

First Church of Christ Scientist
G—corner 8th and C, Coronado (intact)

1929

School for South Bay Union School District
S & G—San Diego County (not built)

Carlsbad Laundry Building
G—Carlsbad (built?)

1929-31

Fire and Police Station
G—corner 3rd and Nevada, Oceanside (nearly intact)

1930-31

Americanization School
G—Division and Center, Oceanside (under restoration)

1931

Kindergarten
G—Nevada St., Oceanside (gone)

Store Building
G—Carlsbad (not built)

1932

Apartment addition to Wheeler Bailey residence
G—7964 Princess, La Jolla (intact)

Guest cottage for Wheeler Bailey
G—7964 Princess, La Jolla (not built)

Assumption of the Blessed Virgin Mary Church
G—Rancho Barona Reservation, Lakeside (remodeled)

1932-33

Twelve cottages for Barona Indian Resettlement
G—Rancho Barona Reservation, Lakeside (some intact)

1934

Oceanside City Hall
G—corner 3rd and Ditmar, Oceanside (intact)

1934

Spanish Village
G—Carlsbad (not built)

1935

Recreation Palace*
G—Oceanside (not built)

Auditorium
G—Oceanside (not built)

Swimming Pool
G—Oceanside (not built)

Veterans' Memorial Building
G—San Diego (not built)

1936

"Glazed Tower," San Diego Administration Building
G—San Diego (not built)

Beauty Parlor*
G—311 S. Elena, Redondo Beach

Zara Witkin Theatre
G—Hollywood (built?)

Blade-Tribune and News Building
G—Tremont (at 1st), Oceanside (nearly intact)

Selected Bibliography

PERIODICAL SOURCES CONTEMPORARY WITH GILL

The Architect and Engineer

January 1913. "Concrete Cottages in California." Vol. 31, pp. 67-72 (article about Lewis Court, Sierra Madre).

May 1915. "Concrete Floors in Dwelling Houses." Vol. 41, pp. 121-123 (letter from Homer Laughlin, Jr., recounting his experience with concrete floors).

March 1916. Irving J. Gill, "New Ideas About Concrete Floors." Vol. 44, pp. 81-83 (abstract of article in *Sunset*).

April 1918. "An Electrically Equipped Home in Pasadena." Vol. 53, p. 39 (article about the West Adams Villa apartments, Pasadena).

June 1919. "Garden Apartment-Houses of the West." Vol. 57, pp. 73-77 (article about Lewis Court, Sierra Madre).

November 1936. Irving Gill obituary, Vol. 124, p. 65.

Architectural Record

October 1912. "Portfolio of Current Architecture." Vol. 32, No. 4, pp. 374-76 (plans and photographs of Laughlin house).

December 1913. Eloise M. Roorbach, "The Garden Apartments of California." Vol. 34, No. 6, pp. 520-30.

Bungalow Magazine

1916. Persis Bingham, "Ruddy Bungalow, Los Angeles, Sanitary House, Rooms Reversed Bring Garden Nearer Home." Vol. 5, pp. 492-99.

The Craftsman

August 1912. Eloise M. Roorbach, "A New Architecture in a New Land." Vol. 22, No. 5, pp. 465-473 (article about Lewis Court, Sierra Madre).

July 1913. Eloise M. Roorbach, "Outdoor Life in California Houses, as Expressed in the New Architecture of Irving J. Gill." Vol. 24, No. 4, pp. 435-439 (article about the Henry H. Timken residence, San Diego).

January 1914. Natalie Curtis, "A New Type of Architecture in the Southwest." Vol. 25, No. 4, pp. 330-335 (article about the Wheeler J. Bailey residence, La Jolla).

May 1914. Eloise M. Roorbach, "Vine-Clad Doorways, Old and New." Vol. 26, No. 2, pp. 179-185 (not specifically about Gill, but illustrated with Gill buildings).

September 1914. "The Bishop's School for Girls: A Progressive Departure from Traditional Architecture." Vol. 26, No. 6, pp. 653-656.

February 1915. "A House with a Garden Room." Vol. 27, No. 5, pp. 564-566 (article about the Thomas Hamilton residence in San Diego, identified as the Mrs. G. Taylor Fulford house).

May 1916. Irving J. Gill, "The Home of the Future: The New Architecture of the West: Small Homes for a Great Country." Vol. 30, No. 2, pp. 140-151, 220 (article in which Gill expresses his personal theories about architecture).

House and Garden

July 1914. Bertha H. Smith, "Creating an American Style of Architecture." Vol. 26, pp. 17-20, 46.

House Beautiful

March 1902. Hazel W. Waterman, "A Granite Cottage in California." Vol. 11, No. 4, pp. 244-253 (article about the Waldo & Hazel Waterman residence, San Diego; Hebbard & Gill not mentioned).

September 1914. Eloise M. Roorbach, "A House of Individuality." Vol. 36, No. 4, pp. 112-113 (article about Paul Miltimore residence in Pasadena).

November 1914. Eloise M. Roorbach, "The Arch in Domestic Architecture." Vol. 26, pp. 186-188.

February 1921. "California House of Distinguished Simplicity." Vol. 49, pp. 94-95 (article about Walter L. Dodge house).

Independent

August 28, 1913. "Concrete Curves and Cubes." Vol. 75, pp. 515-516 (article about Lewis Court, Sierra Madre).

Keith's Magazine

May 1917. Henry K. Pierson, "Homes They Build in San Diego" Vol. 37, No. 5, pp. 321-25 (article illustrated with Gill buildings but Gill not mentioned).

October 1917. "Pre-Cast Walls for the Concrete House." Vol. 38, No. 10, pp. 223-26 (article about the Aiken method used in the tilt-slab construction of the Mary Banning residence, Los Angeles).

Southwest Builder and Contractor

October 16, 1936. "Architect Irving J. Gill: Exponent of Simplified Design Passes Away." Vol. 88, p. 12.

Southwest Contractor and Manufacturer

November 22, 1913. "A House Whose Walls were Built on a Table." pp. 8-9 (article on the Mary Banning residence, Los Angeles).

Sunset Magazine

March 1913. Walter Willard, "Moving the Factory Back to the Land." Vol. 30, pp. 299-304 (article about Torrance).

August 1915. Bertha H. Smith, "California's First Cubist House." Vol. 35, pp. 368-376 (article about the Mary Banning residence, Los Angeles).

December 1915. Irving J. Gill, "New Ideas About Concrete Floors." Vol. 35, pp. 1164-1168.

Technical World Magazine

August 1911. C. L. Edholm, "Beautiful Fountain at San Diego." pp. 723-724 (article about the fountain at Horton Plaza, San Diego).

April 1914. "Architect in Secession." Vol. 21, pp. 231-232 (brief article about Gill's quest for simplicity).

The Touchstone

January 1921. "California Architecture Showing Moorish Feeling." Vol. 8, No. 4, pp. 286-292 (article illustrated mostly with Irving Gill buildings credited to Louis Gill).

Vogue

October 15, 1916. Vol. 48 (article about the Walter Dodge residence, Los Angeles).

Western Architect

April 1913. Eloise Roorbach, "Celebrating Simplicity in Architecture." Vol. 19, pp. 35-41.

ADDITIONAL SOURCES CONTEMPORARY WITH GILL

Hitchcock, Jr., Henry-Russell. "Wright and the International Style." In *Art in America in Modern Times*, eds. Holger Cahill and Alfred H. Barr. New York: Museum of Modern Art, 1934. pp. 70-72.

International News Service. "Irving J. Gill." In *Press Reference Library, Notables of the West*. New York: 1913.

James, George Wharton. "California's Domestic Architecture." In *California Romantic and Beautiful*. Boston: The Page Company, 1914.

RECENT BIBLIOGRAPHIC SOURCES

Britton, James. "The Strength of Irving Gill," "The Weakness of Irving Gill." *San Diego Magazine* 11 (January 1959): 32-41.

Brunet, Jan. "The House on Princess Street." *San Diego Magazine* 17 (August 1965): 52-55 (article about Wheeler J. Bailey house).

Ferris, Helen McElfresh. "Irving John Gill: San Diego Architect." *Journal of San Diego History* 17 (Fall 1971): 1-19.

Flanigan, Kathleen. "William Sterling Hebbard: Consumate San Diego Architect." *Journal of San Diego History* 33 (Winter 1987): 1-42.

Gebhard, David. "Irving Gill." In *California Design 1910*, eds. Timothy J. Anderson, Eudorah M. Moore, and Robert W. Winter. Pasadena: California Design Publications, 1974.

Gebhard, David and Bruce Kamerling. "Irving J. Gill." In *Master Builders*. National Trust for Historic Preservation, 1985.

Irene (Atkinson), Janet. "Irving Gill." Unpublished graduate thesis, school not identified, no date but contains research letters dated 1975, copy at San Diego Historical Society, Research Archives.

Jacyl. "Irving Gill the Architect." *San Diego Magazine* 22 (November 1969): 66-75.

Jordy, William H. "Craftsmanship as Reductive Simplification: Irving Gill's Dodge House." Chap. in *American Buildings and Their Architects, Progressive and Academic Ideals at the Turn of the Twentieth Century*. Garden City, New York: Anchor Press/Doubleday, 1976.

Kamerling, Bruce. "Irving Gill: The Artist as Architect." *Journal of San Diego History* 15 (Spring 1979): 151-190.

_____. "Hebbard & Gill, Architects," "George White & Anna Gunn Marston House," "Self-Guided Walking Tour of Seventh Avenue." *Journal of San Diego History* 36 (Spring/Summer 1990).

Kroll, Rev. C. Douglas. "Louis John Gill: Famous But Forgotten Architect." *Journal of San Diego History* 30 (Summer 1984): 153-166.

McCoy, Esther. "Gill, Irving." In *Macmillan Encyclopedia of Architects*, ed. Adolf K. Placzek. New York: The Free Press (Macmillan), 1982.

_____. "Irving Gill." In *California Design 1910*, eds. Timothy J. Anderson, Eudorah M. Moore, and Robert Winter. Pasadena: California Design Publications, 1974.

_____. "Irving Gill." In *Five California Architects*. New York: Reinhold Publishing Corp., 1962.

_____. *Irving Gill, 1870-1936*. Los Angeles: Los Angeles County Museum, 1958 (exhibition catalogue).

Mitchell, Thomas W. *Reviewing the Vision, A Story of the Bishop's School*. La Jolla: 1979.

Montes, Gregory. "Balboa Park, 1909-1911, The Rise and Fall of the Olmsted Plan." *Journal of San Diego History* 28 (Winter 1982): 46-67.

Trapp, Kenneth R., et al. *The Arts and Crafts Movement in California: Living the Good Life*. Oakland: The Oakland Museum, 1993.

University of San Diego, Department of History, Graduate Division. *San Diego Architects 1868-1939*. San Diego: University of San Diego, 1991.

ARCHIVAL SOURCES

Bertram Goodhue Collection, Avery Architectural Library, Columbia University, New York, NY.

Esther McCoy Papers, Archives of American Art, Smithsonian Institution, including:

> Horatio Warren Bishop to Esther McCoy, 13 May 1966, 15 pages handwritten reminiscences of Gill.

> Irving John Gill, handwritten journal kept toward the end of his life.

> Louis J. Gill, "Irving J. Gill," typescript manuscript for a speech, 9 pages, dated October, 1958.

Olmsted Archives, Frederick Law Olmsted National Historic Site, National Park Service, Brookline, MA.

Marvin Rand & Associates, Venice, California (extensive photographic record of Gill buildings taken from the 1950s to the present).

San Diego Historical Society, Architectural Records Collection (contains some original Irving Gill and Louis Gill drawings and original blueprints).

San Diego Historical Society, Photograph Collection (extensive collection of historical photographs of Gill buildings).

University of California, Santa Barbara, University Art Museum, Architectural Drawing Collection (extensive holdings of original Irving Gill and Louis Gill drawings, photographs, etc.).

Index

About the Author

Bruce Kamerling has been employed by the San Diego Historical Society since 1977 and has held the position of Curator of Collections since 1980. An honorary life member of the Save Our Heritage Organisation, he served four years as a director including one term as president. He sat on the City of San Diego's Historical Site Board from 1983 to 1988 and served as a trustee of the Balboa Art Conservation Center from 1981 to 1993. In 1988, he was placed in charge of the restoration and furnishing of Hebbard & Gill's Marston House for use as a public museum. Kamerling has written numerous articles on San Diego's cultural history, and the Historical Society published his book, *100 Years of Art in San Diego* in 1991. He prepared the San Diego section for *The Arts and Crafts Movement in California, Living the Good Life*, published by the Oakland Museum in 1993.